the
REBUILT WOMAN

THE REBUILT SERIES™

Book 1 — The Rebuilt Woman — Emerald Edition
Book 2 — The Rebuilt Soul — Gold Edition
Book 3 — The Rebuilt Leader — Onyx Edition
Book 4 — The Rebuilt Legacy — Diamond Edition

PLUS:
The Rebuilt Man — Iron Edition

Go to: The Rebuilt Series Channel

EMERALD EDITION
the
REBUILT WOMAN

By Dawn Williams-
Licensed Therapist & Social Worker Specializing in Healing Trauma and Realeasing Leaders

COPYRIGHT PAGE

© 2025 Dawn Williams
All rights reserved. No part of this book may be reproduced, stored, or transmitted in any form or by any means — electronic, mechanical, photocopying, recording, or otherwise — without prior written permission from the author.
This book contains personal experiences blended with therapeutic insights. It is intended for inspiration, education, and emotional support. It is not a substitute for professional medical, psychological, legal, or financial advice.

ISBN (Softcover): 9781764378031
ISBN (Hardcover): 9781764378024
Editor: Chelsea Wilcox
Published by: KMD BOOKS PTY LTD
Printed in Australia.

Dedication

To my four beautiful daughters

Summer, Ella, Gracie, and Jada.

You are the reason I found the courage to rise,

the reason I chose healing over silence,

and the reason I decided to break the cycle once and for all.

Every step I've taken, every tear I've cried,

and every victory I've claimed has been for you.

I want you to grow into women who know their worth,

who recognise real love,

and who never settle for the kind of pain I once carried.

May this book be a reminder that

your story can always be rewritten,

your voice always matters,

and you come from a woman who rebuilt herself

so you would never have to.

With all my love,

Mum. xx

"What tried to break you became the very thing that built you."
Dawn

THE REBUILT WOMAN

THE REBUILT WOMAN™ DISCLAIMER

A gentle reminder and a professional boundary
This book, course and all related content are created to inform, inspire, and support your healing journey. While I am a certified counsellor, psychotherapist, and a student of Social Work, the material shared here is not a substitute for professional medical, psychological, legal, or financial advice.
I speak from lived experience, clinical training, and years of working with women in trauma recovery. Every tool, reflection, and strategy is offered to empower you — but your healing journey is unique, and what works for one person may not be right for another.

Please seek the guidance of a qualified health professional if you are experiencing acute distress, mental health concerns, domestic violence, or crisis.
If you are in immediate danger,
contact emergency services in your area.

By engaging with this content, you acknowledge that you are responsible for your own wellbeing, choices, and actions. Healing is personal — and you have full permission to take what resonates, leave what doesn't, and move at the pace that feels right for you.
You are not alone.
You are rebuilding.
You are rising.

Dawn

the REBUILT WOMAN

TABLE OF CONTENTS

Part 1: The Descent – Recognizing the Signs
Chapter 1: The Perfect Beginning
How the relationship started—charm, love bombing, dreams of a future.

Chapter 2: Walking on Eggshells
The slow erosion of self-worth—first red flags, self-doubt, emotional control.

Part 2: The Breaking Point – Finding the Courage to Leave
Chapter 3: When Love Turns to Fear
The shift—control tightening, verbal and emotional abuse escalating.

Chapter 4: Trapped in the Storm
Why leaving wasn't simple—fear, financial control, isolation.

Chapter 5: The Moment I Knew
The breaking point—what finally made you decide to leave.

Chapter 6: Planning My Escape
How you prepared, the obstacles you faced, the fears that almost stopped you.

Part 3: The Aftermath – Healing & Rediscovering Yourself
Chapter 7: The Aftermath: The Reality of Leaving
Emotional whiplash, grief, relief, and the unexpected struggles of starting over.

Chapter 8: Facing the Trauma
Processing what happened, struggling with guilt, shame, and PTSD.

Chapter 9: Reclaiming My Power
The small but powerful steps you took to rebuild confidence.

Chapter 10: Learning to Trust Again
The fear of relationships, friendships, and allowing love back into your life.

Part 4: The Transformation – A New Beginning
Chapter 11: Finding My Purpose
How your pain turned into purpose (e.g., advocacy, faith, new dreams).

Chapter 12: You Are Not Alone
A final message of hope—what you wish someone had told you in your darkest moments.

Bonus Resources:
- 90-Day Scripture Plan for Healing
- Next Steps - Join the Movement
- A list of support resources (hotlines, shelters, legal aid, therapy options)

EMERALD EDITION

She rises from the ashes,
not as who she was,
but as who she was always meant to become.

Emerald light covers her—
the colour of rebirth,
of healing,
of a heart reclaimed.

Where she once felt broken,
God is weaving wholeness.
Where pain once lived,
purpose now awakens.
Where silence once protected her,
her voice now restores her.

The phoenix within her stretches its wings,
new strength forming where old wounds once lived.
Fire did not destroy her—
it refined her.

She is the woman rebuilt.
The woman remembered by heaven.
The woman rising with wisdom in her scars
and glory in her eyes.

She is emerald—
renewed.
restored.
reborn.
She is phoenix—
ascending from what tried to end her.

And now,
with God's presence surrounding her
like a rainbow of promise,
she steps forward—

not in fear,
but in fire.
Not in pieces,
but in power.
Not as the old version of herself,
but as the woman she was always destined to be.

She is the Rebuilt Woman.
And her rising begins now.

THE REBUILT WOMAN

INTRODUCTION

Rebuilding: A Journey Toward Freedom and Healing

There was a time when I wanted this story to stay buried—hidden in the corners of my heart, known only to a few close people. I believed that keeping it to myself would somehow protect others and shield me from the pain of reliving it. But today, as a mother of four incredible daughters, I can no longer remain silent. I refuse to let them follow in my footsteps, repeating the same generational patterns of dysfunction. I want them to know there is a way out—a way to break free and rewrite their story.

This book is my way of doing just that. It's my offering to you—a testimony of survival, healing, and rising above the darkness that once held me captive. But this isn't just my story. It's a story that echoes through the lives of so many—one of struggle, strength, and ultimately, redemption.

The truth is, I once wished this chapter of my life would remain unspoken, a whisper of the past. But now, I feel a deep, undeniable calling. I believe God has led me to share my journey, hoping it will light the way for someone still caught in the storm. This book is for those who feel alone in their suffering, for those who have been taught to doubt their worth, for those who have endured abuse and manipulation yet still long for healing and peace.

I want you to know—you are not alone. I see you. I hear you. And I am living proof that you can break free and change the course of your life. You can rise from the ashes and rebuild yourself stronger than before.

If my story helps even one woman see herself differently—to recognize that she is worthy of love, respect, and peace—then every tear I've shed and every painful step I've taken will have been worth it. Together, we can end the cycles of abuse and dysfunction. Together, we can heal and reclaim the beautiful lives we were meant to live.

This book is more than a personal journey; it's a call to action. A call to break free, to heal, and to find hope again.

Domestic violence is a silent epidemic

1 in 3 women globally will experience violence

Domestic violence is a silent epidemic, affecting millions of people worldwide. It knows no boundaries—crossing gender, age, race, and socioeconomic status—leaving deep and lasting scars on its victims. Yet, many suffer in silence, trapped by fear, shame, and the relentless grip of coercive control.

Consider these staggering statistics:

- 1 in 3 women globally will experience physical or sexual violence in their lifetime, most often at the hands of someone they know (WHO).
- In the United States, a woman is assaulted or beaten every 9 seconds (NCADV).
- 1 in 7 men have been victims of severe physical violence by an intimate partner (CDC).
- Domestic violence accounts for 15% of all violent crime annually (Bureau of Justice Statistics).

These numbers represent more than just data—they tell the stories of real people who have endured unimaginable pain, often in silence. You may be one of them, or you may know someone who is.

"I was only 15 when I started dating him. He was charming at first, then he became controlling. He would tell me who I could talk to, what I could wear, and even where I could go. I thought it was normal until my friend pointed out the signs of emotional abuse. At 18, I finally got out. I'm now in college, studying to become a counselor to help others who were in my shoes." — Chloe, 18

What readers can expect

This book is a beacon of hope, a guide for those who feel trapped, and a call to action for society to confront this pervasive issue. As a survivor of domestic violence, I have lived through the confusion, fear, and self-doubt that so many endure. But I also know the power of healing and the freedom that comes from reclaiming your life.

Healing is not a straight path, and the journey can feel overwhelming. However, every step—no matter how small—moves you closer to independence, self-worth, and lasting peace.

In the pages ahead, you will find:

- **Insight** into the patterns and impact of abuse.
- **Tools** for self-reflection, healing, and empowerment.
- **Story of resilience** to remind you that you are not alone.

By picking up this book, you've already taken the first step toward change. Together, we will explore how to break free, heal, and rebuild your life.

This book will help you:

- **Recognize** the patterns and cycles.
- **Understand** the emotional toll of abuse and its aftermath.
- **Develop** tools for self-reflection, healing, and empowerment.

As we walk this journey together, we'll navigate the complex emotions, challenges, and triumphs that come with reclaiming your life. You are not alone, and there is hope.

the REBUILT WOMAN

Stage 1: The Descent – Recognizing the Signs

CHAPTER 1
The Perfect Beginning

It felt surreal—a whirlwind romance that swept me off my feet and made me believe in love again. From the moment we met, he was everything I had ever dreamed of—kind, attentive, and irresistibly charming. He listened to me in a way no one ever had before, as if I were the most important person in the world. His affection was overwhelming, and for the first time in my life, I felt truly seen. It was everything I had ever wanted, and I couldn't help but fall for it. He called me constantly, sent sweet messages, and showered me with compliments. "You're the one I've been waiting for," he would say, making me feel as if I had been hand-picked just for him. His promises of a bright future together were so vivid, so real—I could see it, too.

He spoke of marriage, of children, of the adventures we would take. It was a dream come true.

But it wasn't just his words; his actions made me believe in the fantasy. He was thoughtful, always looking for ways to make my life easier—folding my laundry without being asked, anticipating my needs before I even voiced them.

The Perfect Beginning

"deep inside, there was a quiet voice, a small whisper of doubt"

He was affectionate, always reaching for my hand, pulling me into warm embraces, making me feel safe. He was adventurous, always planning little trips and experiences, painting a picture of a life together that was exciting and full of possibility.

He was chatty and social, effortlessly charming everyone around him, and I loved that about him. He made me feel like we belonged together, like we were a team. "You're my real family," he would say, making me feel chosen in a way I had never felt before.

Within months, we had moved in together. It felt fast, but I reassured myself—when love is real, why wait?

Yet, deep inside, a quiet voice whispered doubts. There was something too perfect about it all—too much love, too much attention, too much... of everything. But I pushed those thoughts aside, convincing myself I was just being skeptical. This was love. Real love. I was completely addicted to his love.

What is love bombing ?

It took me a while to understand, but looking back, I now know that what I experienced was love bombing—a tactic often used by abusers to manipulate and control their victims. Love bombing is when someone showers you with excessive affection, praise, and attention to win your trust and make you emotionally dependent on them. It feels incredible at first, but it isn't genuine love. It's manipulation, a way to draw you in so they can later control you.

I thought it was real love. After all, he made me feel special, important, and desired. How could that be anything but love? But love bombing is a strategy that disguises control, and I didn't realize I was being set up for something much darker.

Recognizing the Signs

The Seduction Before the Storm

At the time, I didn't realize how quickly things could change. I remember the first time he said something offhandedly that didn't quite sit right with me. It was subtle—a tone in his voice that made me freeze. The air seemed to shift, and suddenly, I wasn't sure where I stood. But just as quickly, he would shower me with affection again, making me forget the unease.

The cycle continued—moments of love and attention, followed by coldness or subtle anger. But I was so caught up in the affection, so wrapped up in the dream of our future together, that I ignored the signs. I convinced myself that if I loved him more, if I gave more of myself, the relationship would be perfect. If I just prayed enough, tried harder—maybe I could make it work. I begged God for strength, patience, and wisdom. Please, God, help me make this work.

But deep down, I knew the peace I felt was temporary. The love bombing was the seduction before the storm, and I was too deep in the illusion to see it.

One night, we went out with a group of friends, drinking and having fun. At some point, we got separated, and I decided to take a cab back to our place alone. Later, I heard the others arriving, laughing and chatting as they walked toward the house. For a joke, I hid in the bushes, thinking it would be funny to scare them when they got closer. But as I crouched there, I overheard my partner's voice, sharp with anger: "She's going to get a hiding for leaving."

Recognizing the Signs

"He just snapped"

I froze. My heart pounded in my chest, and my breath caught in my throat. He sounded furious. I had never heard him talk about me like that before. Was he serious? Panic took over. I knew I couldn't stay. Fear gripped me as I scrambled from the bushes, my hands shaking as I fumbled for my car keys. I jumped into my car and sped off, trying to process what I had just heard. But before I could even make sense of it, before I could fully register the danger I was in, the reality hit—hard. A fist came through the car window. A punch—straight to my nose. Shock. Pain. Disbelief. Everything around me blurred, my mind struggling to catch up with what had just happened. Did that really just happen? The man who had once promised to love and cherish me had just struck me in a way that shattered every illusion I had held onto. But he just snapped. I wanted to believe it was a mistake. That he hadn't meant it. That somehow, this wasn't what it seemed. But deep down, I knew. The mask had slipped. And nothing would ever be the same again.

I wanted to believe it was a mistake. That he hadn't meant it. That somehow, this wasn't what it seemed. But deep down, I knew. The mask had slipped. And nothing would ever be the same again.

Recognizing the Signs

Why I Stayed: The Patterns I Didn't See

For a long time, I couldn't understand why I stayed—why I ignored the red flags, made excuses, and convinced myself that love meant enduring pain. But when I finally looked back, I saw the truth—this wasn't just about him. It was about me. About the patterns ingrained in me since childhood.

I grew up in a home where love and pain existed in the same breath, where I had to tiptoe around emotions, predict moods, and adjust myself to keep the peace. I learned to be unseen, to withdraw for safety. I understood early on that love wasn't always safe—that it could turn sharp without warning. In many ways, I had been prepared for this relationship long before it even began.

Familiar Chaos
When I met him, he was everything I had dreamed of—affectionate, attentive, and always present. He listened like no one ever had. He made me feel like the most important person in the world.

But love shouldn't feel like being swept away—it should feel like standing firm.
I didn't know that then.

The first time he snapped at me, something inside me froze. I recognized that tone, that shift in the air. It was the same feeling I had as a child when I sensed a storm coming. I had spent years learning how to avoid outbursts, how to make myself small enough to stay safe.

So when his anger flared, I did what I had always done—I adjusted. I soothed him. I told myself it wasn't that bad.

And when he came back with apologies and promises, I forgave him.
I had seen this cycle before, but I didn't call it abuse.
I called it love.

Recognizing the Signs

Minimizing the Pain

I shared earlier when he first truly scared me—his voice, laced with anger, muttering that I was "going to get a hiding for leaving." My stomach dropped. My body tensed. But I convinced myself I had misheard him.

Yet my reaction betrayed the truth—I ran, I hid, I withdrew. I drove off in a panic. But before I could escape, a punch landed on my nose.

In that moment, the man who once felt like my love, my safe place, became my greatest fear.

And yet, I still stayed.

The Lies I Told Myself

- It was just the alcohol talking.
- He just had the wrong idea about me.
- It wasn't that bad.
- At least he apologized.
- He loves me. He's just hurt.

These weren't truths. These were the survival instincts of a little girl trained to endure. A girl who had been taught that love meant sacrifice. Who had learned that pain was just part of the package.

A Survivor

"I spent 15 years in a marriage that slowly broke me down. He told me I wasn't good enough, I couldn't manage without him. For years, I believed it. But when my children started asking questions about why I was sad all the time, I knew I had to leave. At 47, I finally found the strength to step away. It's been a long road, but now I'm living my truth." — Linda, 47

Why Victims Stay

The decision to stay in an abusive relationship is complex. Fear, love, manipulation, and hope often cloud judgment. Society's misconceptions—like asking, "Why didn't you just leave?"—further isolate victims.

Many women remain in abusive relationships due to a range of complex factors that often go unnoticed by others. **Up to 99% of survivors** experience financial abuse, leaving them without the resources to leave safely. Fear of retaliation is another major barrier—**75% of victims** who attempt to leave report facing increased threats or violence, and up to 20% of domestic violence homicides occur within the first two days of leaving.

Emotional manipulation, including gaslighting and trauma bonding, keeps victims doubting their reality and psychologically tied to their abuser. On average, it takes a **victim seven attempts** to leave before breaking free permanently. For mothers, concerns about their children's safety and custody weigh heavily—**31%** stay out of fear of losing custody, while others worry that leaving will expose their children to escalated violence.

Isolation is another key factor, as abusers often sever victims' ties to friends, family, and community. **One in three victims** report feeling they have no one to turn to. Cultural and religious pressures, along with societal stigma, can create additional obstacles—**42% of women** in some communities stay due to fear of judgment or pressure to keep the family intact.

Understanding these dynamics and the risks survivors face is crucial to offering support without judgment and helping them find the resources and strength to rebuild their lives.

Key Insight

Leaving an abusive relationship is not as simple as "just walking away." Fear, financial dependence, love, hope, manipulation, and societal barriers all play a role. Understanding these dynamics fosters empathy and helps survivors find support without judgment.

Recognizing the Signs

Breaking the Cycle

Breaking the cycle wasn't just about leaving—it was about learning to live again. At first, I didn't even realize I was trapped. I thought if I loved harder, prayed more, or became the perfect partner, things would change. But no matter how much I gave, the cycle continued: affection followed by tension, followed by explosion, and then the apologies that made me believe it would be different next time. It never was. The day I finally asked myself, *Why am I staying?* instead of *Why is this happening to me?* was the day everything began to shift.

If you're reading this and feeling stuck, I want you to know this: you don't have to stay in the cycle. You don't have to prove your love by enduring suffering. Fear is not love. Control is not love. You are worthy of safety, peace, and a love that doesn't leave you feeling broken. If you're not ready to leave today, that's okay—start by recognizing the truth. Start by believing you deserve better. And when you're ready, take that first step, no matter how small. I promise you, there is life beyond the pain. There is healing. And you are not alone.

Recognizing the Signs

Recognizing the Red Flags

If you're in a relationship that feels too good to be true, trust your instincts. There's a difference between the excitement of love and the suffocating grip of manipulation. The early stages of a relationship should feel exhilarating, but they shouldn't leave you feeling overwhelmed or dependent. If you find yourself walking on eggshells, constantly questioning your partner's mood, or feeling anxious about their reactions, these are red flags that something isn't right.

Here are a few things to consider:

- **If it feels rushed:** Abusers often try to push the relationship forward too quickly, creating a sense of urgency that makes you feel like you have to keep up with their intense affection. Healthy relationships develop at a natural pace, allowing both partners to build trust and connection over time.

- **If it feels like you're the center of their world:** While it might seem flattering at first, an unhealthy dynamic often emerges when one partner makes you feel like the only important person in their life. This can be a tactic to isolate you from others and gain control over your world. In a balanced relationship, both partners share the focus and maintain their individuality.

- **If you feel overwhelmed by their affection:** Love bombing—excessive flattery, gifts, and attention—can feel intoxicating but is often a manipulation tactic. Healthy love is consistent, respectful, and allows both partners the space to breathe and grow independently.

A Letter to You

I know what it's like to get lost in the illusion of a perfect beginning—to believe you've found the love of your life, only to be blindsided by manipulation and control. If you're reading this and wondering whether you're in a relationship where the love feels too intense, too perfect, or even too controlling, I want you to hear this loud and clear: You are not crazy. You are not weak. You are not unworthy of real love.

God created you to be cherished, valued, and to live a life filled with peace. He never intended for you to live in fear, to feel like you must earn love through sacrifice or pain. The love you deserve is one that uplifts you, one that makes you feel seen, heard, and safe.

If you find yourself questioning the foundation of your relationship, take a step back. Listen to your heart. Listen to your faith. Listen to that quiet voice inside telling you something isn't right. You are worthy of peace, and you are worthy of a love free from manipulation and fear.

Start by holding onto this truth: You deserve to be loved for who you are, not for what you can give. And remember, God is with you every step of the way, guiding you toward the life and love you were always meant to have.

Dawn Williams

JOURNAL PROMPT:

Reflection

1. Think back to the beginning of your relationship.
2. What red flags did you ignore or explain away?
3. What did you believe love was at the time?

My Triggers:
_____
_____
_____
_____
_____

What did I see but ignored:
_____
_____
_____

Why did I ignore the signs?
_____
_____
_____

What did I believe love was?
_____
_____
_____

Affirmation: I deserve love that is kind, patient, and safe.

Prayer: Lord, help me to see love through Your eyes. Teach me to recognize true love and to release any illusions that have kept me trapped. Heal the parts of me that longed for love in the wrong places. Amen.

the REBUILT WOMAN

Stage 1: The Descent – Recognizing the Signs

CHAPTER 2

Walking on Eggshells I became an expert at predicting the storm before it arrived. The way he walked into the house, the look on his face, the heaviness in the air around him—it all told me what kind of night it would be. I lived in a world of invisible landmines, careful with every word, every breath, every movement. It wasn't just fear; it was survival.

There were moments of seduction, times when I let myself believe that maybe, this time, things would change. But the seduction was never real—it was just the pause before the next explosion. I convinced myself that if I just tried harder, if I just loved more, if I just prayed enough, I could keep the peace. I begged God for strength, for patience, for him to see me, to love me the way I so desperately needed. But the more I gave, the more I lost myself.

The violence began just three months into our relationship. I still remember the shock of that first punch to my nose, delivered through a car window. The physical pain was fleeting compared to the emotional wound it left behind. And yet, instead of leaving, I stayed. I told myself it was a one-time thing, that he didn't mean it, that stress, alcohol, or a bad day had caused it. I made excuses for him the way I had learned to make excuses for people my whole life.

Walking on Eggshells

He withdrew not only from me but from our family. His presence in the home felt like a shadow—there, but unreachable. Conversations became scarce, affection nonexistent, and I was left navigating a marriage that felt more like solitary confinement. His silence could cut deeper than words ever could. The rejection, the coldness, the way he could look through me as if I wasn't there—it was a different kind of abuse, one that left me questioning my worth every single day.

I was taking salsa classes, something that made me feel alive again—something that was mine. When the studio announced its annual dance party, I invited my friends and my partner. That night was beautiful—he laughed with my friends, cracked jokes, and played the part of the loving boyfriend perfectly. For a moment, I let myself believe we were happy. But as soon as we left, everything changed.

Without warning, he dragged me to a dark, unseen place and threw me into a ditch. No explanation. No reason. Just rage.

That night, something in me broke. My fear turned to anger, and my response shifted—I started fighting back. But it didn't matter. He was stronger, and his fury was relentless. He threw me down a flight of stairs, and at that moment, I thought I was going to die. I should have left then. I should have run and never looked back.

But the bond had its grip on me. After a short separation, he pulled me back in with sweet words, with promises, with the seduction of the man I had first fallen for.

And so, I stayed. But I was no longer blind to the truth—I knew I was walking on eggshells, balancing on the edge of his next outburst. The question wasn't if it would happen again.

The question was when.

The Psychology of Walking on Eggshells

Psychologists call this trauma bonding—the cycle of highs and lows that keeps victims attached to their abusers. The moments of kindness create hope, while the fear keeps you trapped. Your body lives in a constant state of stress, always anticipating the next emotional blow. This isn't just an emotional response; it's a physiological one. Your nervous system adapts to the chaos, making peace feel unfamiliar—even unsettling.

For me, the ability to endure, to rationalize, to stay, didn't begin with that relationship—it started long before, in my childhood. I had been trained to accept dysfunction as normal, to confuse love with pain, to walk on eggshells as a means of survival. When love came with conditions, when care was unpredictable, I learned to mold myself to the needs of others just to feel safe. If a parent's love was inconsistent, I adapted. If affection could turn to coldness in an instant, I learned to be small, to be quiet, to not upset the balance.

So when I found myself in a relationship that mirrored that same instability, my nervous system recognized it—not as danger, but as home. The emotional highs reminded me of the rare, fleeting moments of love I craved as a child, and the lows felt like something I was built to endure. Instead of seeing the abuse for what it was, my subconscious told me to work harder, to prove my worth, to earn the love I had always longed for.

That's the cruel trick of unresolved childhood wounds—they don't stay in the past. They show up in the present, guiding your choices, shaping your tolerances, whispering that this is the best you'll ever get. Until we face those wounds, we remain vulnerable to relationships that keep us trapped in the same painful cycles.

And so, I stayed—not because I didn't know it was wrong, but because, deep down, a part of me still believed love was something you had to suffer for.

Faith in the Midst of Chaos

I turned to my faith as an anchor. I told myself that love endures, that marriage is a covenant, that God could soften even the hardest heart. *"Love bears all things, believes all things, hopes all things, endures all things."* **(1 Corinthians 13:7)** I clung to that verse, believing that my endurance was a form of love. But what I failed to see was that love should never come at the cost of my own soul.

One night, as I sat alone, staring at the door, waiting for the sound of his footsteps, I whispered a different prayer: Lord, is this the love You intended for me? And in that silence, I felt the answer settle deep in my spirit. Love was not meant to be fear. Love was not meant to be pain. God did not create me to live in the shadows of someone else's rage.

I remember listening to *It Is Well with My Soul* on repeat. It was the only thing that could soothe my anxious heart.

Breaking the Cycle

If you've ever found yourself monitoring every move, reading every expression, trying to avoid the next outburst—you are not alone. Recognizing the pattern is the first step to breaking it. Here are some truths to hold onto:

- **Love should not feel like a battlefield.** If you're constantly in fight-or-flight mode, something is wrong.
- **Fear is not love.** If your heart races at the sound of their voice in a way that isn't from excitement but terror, that is not love.
- **God does not call you to suffer in silence.** He calls you to peace, to safety, to a life where you are valued and cherished.
- **Your intuition is not lying.** The unease, the anxiety, the gut feeling that tells you something isn't right—listen to it.

Study Spotlight: Adverse Childhood Experiences (ACE)

"The CDC's Adverse Childhood Experiences (ACE) Study revealed that children raised in abusive or dysfunctional homes are far more likely to enter abusive relationships as adults. It isn't weakness—it's wiring. When chaos is familiar, we mistake it for love. Healing begins when we break that cycle for ourselves and for the next generation."

Source: Felitti, V. J., Anda, R. F., Nordenberg, D., et al. (1998). Relationship of childhood abuse and household dysfunction to many of the leading causes of death in adults: The Adverse Childhood Experiences (ACE) Study. American Journal of Preventive Medicine, 14(4), 245–258.

A Letter to You

I know what it's like to walk on eggshells, to live in a home that never truly feels like home. But hear me when I say this: You are not crazy. You are not weak. You do not deserve this. God did not create you to live in fear.

If you're still in this place, I want you to start by doing one thing: Write down your truth. No filters, no justifications. Just the truth. Sometimes, seeing it in front of you is the first step to believing it.

You are worthy of peace. You are worthy of safety. And you are not alone.

Dawn Williams

Study Spotlight: Faith & Coping

"Psychologist Kenneth Pargament found that survivors who leaned on prayer, scripture, and faith experienced more resilience and less depression. Faith doesn't erase pain, but it becomes a lifeline. Every prayer you whispered in the dark was a step toward healing."

Source: Pargament, K. I. (1997). The Psychology of Religion and Coping: Theory, Research, Practice. New York: Guilford Press.

JOURNAL PROMPT:

Reflection

1. Describe a time when you felt you had to change yourself to keep the peace.
2. How did that affect your self-worth?

My Thoughts:

_____

_____

_____

_____

_____

_____

Affirmation: I do not have to shrink myself to be loved. I deserve to feel safe in my own home.

Prayer: God, I have lived in fear for too long. Show me the strength You placed inside me. Help me to trust that I was created for more than survival—I was created for peace. Amen.

the REBUILT WOMAN

Stage 1: The Descent – Recognizing the Signs

CHAPTER 3

When Love Turns to Fear

I remember the first time I felt truly afraid. At first, it was subtle—a small change in his tone, a tightening of his jaw. But I sensed it. Something was different. The warm affection I had grown used to was being replaced by something colder, more calculating. The man I had fallen in love with was still there, but his eyes seemed distant, his words sharper. It wasn't long before I realized our relationship was shifting, and it was no longer a safe place.

He began to pick at little things—my clothes, the way I spoke, the way I looked at him. It was as if he were searching for reasons to criticize, to tear me down. I tried to be perfect, to meet his every expectation, but it was never enough. When I attempted to explain myself, his patience wore thin. His voice would rise, and my heart would race, knowing that at any moment, something bigger could happen.

One night, we were staying in an apartment in Brisbane. I had prepared a beautiful meal for him, setting the table with care, eager to make the evening special. We talked, we laughed, and for a moment, it felt normal—like we were okay. As we lay in bed, I still remember the warmth of that fleeting connection.

And then, without warning, it changed.

When Love Turns to Fear

To this day, I don't even remember what I said—if I said anything at all. But suddenly, he flew into a violent rage. His face contorted with fury as he smashed up the room, punching holes in the walls. I barely had time to react before he grabbed a glass and hurled it at my face. The shattering sound filled the room, and for a split second, I thought it had cut me. Miraculously, it hadn't—but the fear that gripped me in that moment left a scar far deeper than any wound ever could.

He stormed out, driving off like a maniac, and I collapsed in a mess of tears, confusion, and disbelief. What had just happened? How had the night gone from laughter to this? I heard the screech of tires as he tore up the street, hitting two road signs on his way out.

The neighbors had heard everything. Before I knew it, the police were calling me. I was shaking as I answered, still trying to process it all. A female police officer spoke to me, her voice steady and kind. She listened, then said something that would change everything for me:

"Putting a domestic violence order on your partner doesn't mean you don't love him. It means it will help to keep you safe."

Her words hit me like a tidal wave. I had never thought of it like that. In my mind, loving him meant protecting him, standing by him, believing he could change. But in that moment, I saw the truth—I had been so consumed with keeping him happy, with making things right, that I hadn't even realized I was in danger.

I had been trapped in a cycle I didn't recognize, a cycle I didn't even know existed.

That night, a seed was planted in my mind—one that would take time to grow but would eventually lead me to the hardest, yet most necessary, decision of my life.

When Love Turns to Fear

The Cycle of Abuse: Tension, Explosion, Honeymoon Phase

Guide: The Cycle of Abuse The cycle of abuse is a pattern that many victims of domestic violence experience.

It often begins with **tension building**—small things that set the abuser off, like a comment or a look. The victim senses the growing tension and feels an increasing sense of fear. During this stage, they try to keep the peace, doing whatever they can to avoid triggering the abuser's anger. This is when the victim is walking on eggshells, constantly on edge, unsure of what might set the abuser off.

Then comes the **explosion**—the breaking point where the abuser releases their anger. This may come in the form of verbal, emotional, or even physical abuse. The victim is left feeling helpless, confused, and terrified. After the explosion, the abuser may retreat, leaving the victim in a state of shock and devastation.

Finally, there's the **honeymoon phase**. This is the moment the abuser reminds the victim of the person they first fell for—apologies, promises to change, and affectionate gestures. The abuser may cry, express deep regret, and swear it will never happen again. For a while, it might seem like things are returning to normal, but it's only temporary. The cycle will repeat, each time becoming more intense and harder to escape.

At first, I couldn't see it. The cycle was insidious. After every explosion, he would apologize, swear he never meant to hurt me, and promise it wouldn't happen again. And for a while, I believed him. During the honeymoon phase, everything seemed perfect again—he would shower me with affection, tell me how much he loved me, and I would convince myself that the worst was behind us.

This time will be different, I thought. This time, he will change. But the tension always built again. The storm would come, and I would be left in the aftermath, walking through life with a cloud hanging over me. No matter how hard I tried, I could never keep the peace long enough. And with every cycle, it became harder to believe that things would ever change.

When Love Turns to Fear

Recognizing the Cycle

If you're in a relationship like this, you may not realize what's happening at first. The honeymoon phase can be so convincing, the promises of change so powerful. But over time, the cycle becomes clear.

The key to breaking free is recognizing the pattern—understanding that the cycle of tension, explosion, and honeymoon isn't love. It's manipulation.

Here are some things to look for:

Tension: Small criticisms, subtle jabs, and growing frustration. You feel like you're walking on eggshells, never sure what might set them off.

Explosion: The moment the tension breaks and the abuser lashes out— verbally, emotionally, or physically. You're left feeling broken, confused, and afraid.

Honeymoon Phase: The abuser apologies, promises to change, and showers you with affection. For a while, you believe things will get better. But the cycle repeats.

Recognizing the cycle is the first step toward breaking free. You are not alone, and you deserve more than empty promises.

Faith in the Midst of Chaos

During these times, I turned to my faith for strength. I prayed for peace, for wisdom, for protection. But no matter how much I prayed, no matter how deeply I loved him, the cycle continued.

I told myself to be patient, believing that love would overcome everything. *"Love endures all things"* **(1 Corinthians 13:7)**, I reminded myself. But what I failed to see was that **love does not endure abuse.** Love does not ask you to stay in a place where you are belittled, hurt, and controlled.

When Love Turns to Fear

One night, after yet another explosion, I whispered a different prayer:

Lord, show me my worth. Show me that I deserve more than this.

In that moment, I felt God's presence in a way I never had before. A quiet realization settled over me—love should never bring fear. Love should never make you feel small, unworthy, or less than.

God had created me for more. For a love that uplifts, not one that diminishes.

Study Spotlight: The Cycle of Abuse

"Dr. Lenore Walker identified what she called the 'Cycle of Violence': tension building, explosion, then a honeymoon phase. Many survivors describe this as living the same nightmare on repeat. If this feels familiar, know that you are not imagining things—this pattern has been studied for decades, and you are not alone in recognizing it."

Source: Walker, L. E. (1979). The Battered Woman. New York: Harper & Row.

A Letter to You

If you're caught in the cycle of abuse, know this: You are not alone. The fear, the uncertainty, the self-doubt—it's all part of the cycle. But it doesn't have to be your reality forever. The first step to breaking free is acknowledging it. Recognize the tension, the explosion and the honeymoon phase. Understand that these are not signs of love—they are signs of control.

You are worthy of a love that does not leave you afraid. A love that values you for who you are. God calls you to peace, to safety, and to a love that is kind, patient, and selfless. If you find yourself in a place where fear reigns, I encourage you to reach out for help. There is a way out of the cycle, and there is a future beyond the storm. You do not have to live in fear. You are strong, and you are worthy of a love that brings peace, not pain. God sees you, and He has more in store for you than the fear that surrounds you now.

Take a deep breath, and know that you are not alone. You can break the cycle, and you will find freedom.

Dawn Williams

JOURNAL PROMPT:

Reflection

Write about a time when you felt the shift in your relationship—the moment when love turned to fear.
- What did that moment teach you?

My Lessons:
_____
_____
_____
_____
_____

What did I see but ignored:
_____
_____

Why did I ignore the signs?
_____
_____

What did I believe love was?
_____
_____

Affirmation: Fear is not love. Love does not hurt, belittle, or control.

Prayer: Lord, help me to see love through Your eyes. Teach me to recognize true love and to release any illusions that have kept me trapped. Heal the parts of me that longed for love in the wrong places. Amen.

the REBUILT WOMAN

Stage 1: The Descent – Recognizing the Signs

CHAPTER 4
Trapped in the Storm

The hardest part wasn't just the fear—though that was overwhelming—it was the feeling that I couldn't leave. No matter how much I knew something was wrong, no matter how many times I prayed for a way out, I couldn't make myself walk away. It was like being trapped in a storm, where the winds of fear and confusion blew so fiercely that I couldn't find my way to safety.

Every time I thought about leaving, fear would flood my mind: fear of what he might do, fear of what would happen to me if I were alone, fear of how I would survive without him.

But more than anything, it was the children that kept me in place. I couldn't imagine life without them, and the thought of taking them away from their father terrified me. I worried about what it would do to them, how it would affect their lives. I felt responsible for keeping the family together, even if it meant sacrificing my own happiness and safety. (*see Study Spotlight: Children's Recovery)

The idea of raising them alone, without the support of their father, was overwhelming. So, I stayed, convincing myself that I was doing it for them, not fully understanding that I was sacrificing my own well-being in the process.

Trapped in the Storm

Then, there was the isolation. Over time, he slowly pulled me away from my family. At first, it was subtle—he'd make little comments about how they didn't understand our relationship or how badly he thought they treated me. "They don't care about you," he would say. And I believed him. I thought no one would be there for me the way he was. So, I distanced myself from everyone I loved. Soon, I had no one left to turn to. It felt like I was completely alone in this fight. There seemed to be no escape, no way out. And in the silence of my isolation, the storm raged on.

The violence stopped—after the Domestic Violence Order (DVO) had been put in place—but things didn't improve immediately. There was a strange sense of calm, but it didn't last long. Soon after, the children came into the picture, and in many ways, they became the focus of my life.

It felt like they were the only thing that kept me grounded, the one thing that could give me purpose in the chaos. But even as a mother, even as someone responsible for raising them, I still couldn't break free.

I was still caught in the cycle of emotional withdrawal, coldness, and fear. The storm had quieted down, but I was still trapped, living in its aftermath.

It wasn't until later that I would begin to realize that breaking free would require more than just escaping the violence—it would require rebuilding my entire life, starting from within.

The emotional wounds were deeper than I could have imagined. It wasn't just the fear of physical harm anymore; it was the fear of losing myself, of never being able to truly live freely, of continuing to carry the weight of the past. To survive, I threw myself into work and the kids—it kept me distracted and in denial. I buried myself in daily routines, in the responsibilities of being a mother, and in the false comfort of staying busy. It was easier to focus on the immediate demands of life than to face the overwhelming emotions I didn't know how to process. In that busyness, I convinced myself that I was doing okay, that if I just kept moving forward, maybe the pain would eventually go away. But deep down, I knew it wasn't that simple.

Understanding Trauma Bonding: Why Victims Stay

Trauma bonding is a psychological phenomenon that often occurs in abusive relationships. It is a strong emotional attachment that develops between the victim and the abuser, despite the harm caused by the abuse. The cycle of abuse—tension, explosion, honeymoon phase—creates an emotional rollercoaster, and over time, victims become emotionally dependent on the abuser. The love and affection during the honeymoon phase become a lifeline, a brief respite from the storm, and the victim clings to it, believing that the abuse will eventually stop.

This emotional attachment is reinforced by the abuser's intermittent kindness and affection, which creates hope that things will improve. The victim becomes confused, unable to see the relationship for what it truly is. They may blame themselves for the abuse, thinking that if they were just better, the abuser wouldn't act this way.

I experienced this firsthand. Every time he was kind, when he promised that things would change, I believed him. *Maybe this time it will be different,* I thought. He knew how to manipulate my emotions, how to make me feel like I was the problem. And because I was isolated from everyone else, I had no one to challenge my perception. He made me feel like the only way to survive was to stay with him, to try harder, to love more.

But deep down, I knew I wasn't the one causing the problems. It was the cycle of abuse that was slowly consuming me, and yet, I couldn't break free. The fear of leaving, of being alone, of not knowing where I would go or how I would survive, kept me rooted in place.

The Grip of Fear and Isolation

Fear was a constant companion, a shadow that loomed over every decision I made. It wasn't just fear of him; it was fear of the unknown. What would happen if I left? Where would I go? How would I support myself? How could I explain to my family and friends that I had stayed for so long?

In the isolation, it was easy to forget who I was before the abuse. I couldn't remember what it felt like to be independent, to make decisions for myself, to feel free. The world outside seemed distant, like a dream I could no longer reach. And so, I stayed—stuck in the storm, trying to find a way to survive.

The Power of Faith in a Broken World

It was my faith that kept me holding on, even when I felt like I was drowning. I prayed for strength, courage, and clarity. Lord, show me the way out. Help me see the path forward. But the answers weren't always clear. There were days when I felt completely lost, when I wondered if maybe this was just my lot in life. Maybe I wasn't meant to be happy. Maybe I wasn't worth more than the abuse. But in those moments of despair, I began to understand that God had a different plan for me. I wasn't meant to live in fear, to stay trapped in a cycle of abuse. He didn't create me to be controlled, to be made small by someone else's anger. *"For I know the plans I have for you,"* says the Lord, *"plans to prosper you and not to harm you, plans to give you a hope and a future."* **(Jeremiah 29:11)**

I began to hold onto this truth—that God had more in store for me than the storm I was in. And even though I didn't know how to leave, I knew I wasn't meant to stay forever. God was with me, even in the darkness, and He was slowly opening my eyes to the possibility of something more.

Study Spotlight: Trauma Bonding

"Psychologists call this trauma bonding. Dr. Patrick Carnes explains that the cycle of abuse—fear, followed by affection, then fear again—actually changes our brain chemistry. Hormones like dopamine and oxytocin make us cling to the brief moments of love, even when pain is constant. If you've ever asked, 'Why did I stay?'—know that your brain was fighting for survival, not betraying you."

Source: Carnes, P. (1997). The Betrayal Bond: Breaking Free of Exploitive Relationships.

Study Spotlight: Children's Recovery

"A study of children exposed to domestic violence showed increased anxiety and difficulties in school—but also incredible resilience when given support. With safe environments, counseling, and love, children can break free of the cycle. Your choice to heal doesn't just restore you—it plants seeds of freedom for your children, too."

Source: Kitzmann, K. M., Gaylord, N. K., Holt, A. R., & Kenny, E. D. (2003). Child witnesses to domestic violence: A meta-analytic review. Journal of Consulting and Clinical Psychology, 71(2), 339–352.

A Letter to You

If you find yourself trapped in the storm, struggling with fear, or financial control, know this: You are not alone. The cycle of abuse, trauma bonding, and fear can make it seem like there is no way out. But I promise you, there is a way forward. There is hope beyond the storm.

Here are some truths to hold onto:

·Fear is not your future. The fear you feel now is temporary. You do not have to live in the grip of fear forever.
·You are worthy of freedom. God created you to live in peace, to be free from manipulation, control, and isolation.
·You are not to blame. The abuse is not your fault. You are not the cause of the anger, the hurt, or the control. ·You are worthy of love and respect. ·Help is available. Reach out. Whether through friends, family, or professional support, there are people who can help you break free from the storm.

If you're struggling to leave, it's okay. Take one step at a time. Trust that God will guide you and that there is a future beyond the pain. You are stronger than you realize, and you are worth fighting for.

Don't stay trapped in the storm any longer. The light is coming, and you are not alone.

Dawn Williams

JOURNAL PROMPT:
Reflection

What fears kept you (or are keeping you) from leaving? How has isolation or financial control played a role?

My Thoughts:

_____

_____

_____

_____

_____

_____

_____

Affirmation: I am not powerless. God has given me wisdom and strength to break free.

Prayer: Father, I feel trapped. Give me wisdom to see a way ou courage to take the first step, and trust in Your plan for my safety and healing. Amen.

THE REBUILT WOMAN

the REBUILT WOMAN

Stage 2: The Breaking Point – Finding the Courage to Leave

There comes a moment in every storm when you can no longer ignore the rising tide. The winds howl louder, the darkness deepens, and you realize that staying in the eye of the storm is no longer an option. For so long, I had lived in fear, hope, and despair, convinced that leaving was impossible. I believed I wasn't strong enough, that I couldn't survive without him. But the truth is, the decision to leave didn't come from a place of strength—it came from a place of brokenness, exhaustion, and the painful realization that I couldn't endure another day in a cage of fear. Leaving wasn't easy. It wasn't a single moment of clarity when everything suddenly fell into place. It was a series of quiet moments —whispers of truth, gentle nudges from God, and the overwhelming realization that I deserved more than the pain I had been living through. The hardest part wasn't just physically leaving—it was mentally and emotionally accepting that I was worthy of something better. I had to believe that my peace, my safety, and my life were worth fighting for. This part of the journey wasn't about perfection; it was about survival. It was about finding the courage to let go and trusting that the unknown was safer than staying in the storm. Though it felt like stepping into darkness, I slowly began to understand that in order to reclaim my life, I had to leave behind everything that had been holding me hostage. This is the part of my story where the chains began to break, and for the first time in a long time, I felt a flicker of hope that I could breathe again. If you're reading this, you may be at your own breaking point. But know this: you are not alone, and you are not without hope. The journey to freedom is hard, but it is possible. This is where the storm begins to lose its power, and the light begins to break through.

the REBUILT WOMAN

Stage 2: The Breaking Point – Finding the Courage to Leave

CHAPTER 5
The Moment I Knew

I can't remember how many nights anxiety and fear gripped me. I would lie in bed, turning over and over in my mind—where was he? What was he doing? My abuse wasn't just about words or actions; it was emotional neglect and abandonment.

The silence was deafening, and the loneliness cut deeper than any wound. I had learned to read the silence, to sense the storm before it arrived. But that night, something in me shifted. The fear that had always been my constant companion was now joined by something new: clarity.

I had spent years on my knees, praying and begging God to heal our marriage. I pleaded for change, for love, for anything to bring healing to us. I believed in the power of faith, in the sanctity of marriage, and in the vows I had made. I convinced myself that if I just prayed harder, if I just loved more, things would get better. But no matter how much I prayed, the pain remained. The neglect deepened. And I found myself drowning in sorrow.

That night, as I sat on the cold floor, I realized that God was answering me—not in the way I had expected, but in the way I needed. He wasn't calling me to endure; He was calling me to rise.

The Moment I Knew

But rising wasn't easy. It took me a long time to seek proper help because, for the longest time, I didn't even realize I needed it. I didn't recognize that I had been trapped in a cycle of abuse, that the life I had normalized was anything but normal. I was just used to it. It was all I had ever known. I had learned how to survive, but I had never learned what it meant to feel safe. I had never known what it was like to be loved without fear.

The way I responded to his abuse—minimizing it, making excuses, trying harder—wasn't just because of him; it was because of everything that had come before him. It was the product of my childhood, the relationships I had seen, and the subconscious belief that this was just how love worked.

Some might call it learned behavior. Others, especially in the church, might call it a generational curse. Whatever you name it, the truth is that dysfunction had been passed down to me. Without realizing it, I was repeating the same patterns I had witnessed as a child. The fear, the silence, the desperate need for love that never quite came—these weren't new to me. They were familiar. And in that familiarity, I stayed, because I didn't know anything else.

Eventually, I couldn't take the torment anymore and sought a counselor. I was completely disillusioned with life, marriage, love, and even God. I poured out my years of pain and confusion, sharing my story with her. And then, I asked a simple, yet profound question that shifted my mindset: "Are all men like this?"

Her answer was straightforward, yet it carried a deep weight: **"No, not all men are like this."**

I felt a strange sense of relief, though disbelief lingered. Up until that moment, I had only known men who abused me—physically, mentally, and emotionally. From my childhood to my marriage, abuse had been a constant. The mental and emotional abuse and neglect I was experiencing now were far worse than anything I had ever known, and I had come to believe this was just the way relationships were.

But her words planted a seed of possibility: maybe, just maybe, there was another way to live. For the first time, I dared to hope that I deserved better.

The Turning Point: Why It Happens

Psychologists call this the "cognitive shift"—the moment when a survivor finally sees the abuse for what it truly is. Sometimes, it's triggered by a particularly violent incident. Other times, it's a quiet realization, a whisper in the soul that says, *This is not love. This is not my life. This is not how my story ends.*

For me, it came when I realized I had become a shell of the person I once was. I looked in the mirror and didn't recognize the woman staring back at me. Where was the girl with dreams? Where was the woman who laughed without fear? That day, I made a choice—not just to leave, but to believe that something better was waiting for me.

Faith and Freedom: A Spiritual Awakening

In that moment of desperation, I cried out to God. Not in a polished prayer, but in raw, broken words. Lord, if You are there, if You see me, show me the way out.

There's a verse in **Isaiah 43:19** that says: *"See, I am doing a new thing! Now it springs up; do you not perceive it? I am making a way in the wilderness and streams in the wasteland."* That promise became my anchor. I didn't have a full plan, but I had a sliver of hope—and sometimes, that's all it takes to start moving forward.

Practical Steps: Preparing for the Next Step

If you are reading this and feel that shift inside you, know we get you! The moment you realize you need to change is both terrifying and empowering. Here are some steps to consider:

- **Acknowledge the Reality** – Write down what has happened. Seeing the truth on paper can break through denial.

- **Seek Support** – A trusted friend, a therapist, or a support group can help you navigate your next steps.
- **Create a Safety Plan** – If leaving immediately isn't safe, start preparing in small ways (setting aside money, gathering important documents, planning a safe place to go).
- **Strengthen Your Faith** – Pray, meditate, and surround yourself with verses, affirmations, or mantras that remind you of your worth.

Practical Steps: Preparing for the Next Step

Speaking out is more than just telling your story—it's breaking the chains of silence that keep so many of us trapped. During this time, the first Rebuilt Woman Healing Circle was born with just two women who dared to share their raw, unfiltered truth. For the first time, we weren't hiding behind forced smiles or pretending things were okay. We spoke the reality of what was happening in our personal lives, and in doing so, we found something powerful—support, accountability, and the kind of healing that only comes from being truly seen.

I want to acknowledge the friends who walked with me on this journey—you know who you are. Because of that first healing circle, lives began to change. Healing happened. Strength was found. And from that moment, The Rebuilt Woman became more than just a personal journey—it became a movement.

I encourage you to find a healing circle of your own. Whether it's The Rebuilt Woman or another safe space, you don't have to walk this journey alone. Details on how to join a Rebuilt Woman Healing Circle—online or in person—can be found at the back of this book. You are worthy of healing, and you are not alone.

A Letter to You

If you're standing at your own breaking point, hear me when I say: You are stronger than you know. You are worthy of peace. You are not alone. The first step is the hardest, but once you take it, you are already walking toward freedom.

What is your moment of knowing? What is the whisper inside of you saying? Listen to it. Trust it. It's leading you home.

Dawn Williams

JOURNAL PROMPT:
Reflection

What was (or is) your breaking point? How did it feel to realize you couldn't stay any longer?

My Thoughts :

_____

_____

_____

_____

_____

_____

_____

·**Affirmation:** Courage is not the absence of fear but taking action despite it. I am brave, I am strong, and I will not let fear keep me in bondage.·

Prayer: Lord, give me the strength to walk away from what no longer serves me. Let me trust that You have something better for me, even if I cannot see it yet. Amen.

the REBUILT WOMAN

Stage 2: The Breaking Point – Finding the Courage to Leave

CHAPTER 6
Planning My Escape

The decision to leave wasn't something that happened overnight. It was a quiet, painful process—one filled with fear, doubts, and endless "what-ifs." I spent days, sometimes weeks, working through my thoughts, trying to understand what it would take to finally break free. It felt like a mountain too high to climb, and every time I looked up, it seemed impossible. But deep down, I knew that the longer I stayed, the more I would lose—my soul, my peace, my dignity.
Everything was being slowly drained from me.

The first obstacle was simple: how do I even begin? The weight of the unknown was crushing. I couldn't just pack a bag and walk out the door—I had to think through every detail. The thought of what he might do if he found out I was planning to leave sent chills down my spine. I had seen his rage before, and the thought of provoking that fear left me paralyzed. What if he found me? What if he hurt me—or worse, my children, my family?

It took three years for me to make the decision to change things, and another year to transition into separation. By 2017, we were officially separated, and I filed for divorce. But before that, I endured years of silent suffering. He refused to eat with us as a family. He would disappear for days, leaving me alone with the children, offering no explanation of where he had gone or when he would return. He was withdrawn, neglectful, sometimes verbally abusive, and financially controlling.

Planning My Escape

He spent money on luxuries and things that served only his needs, while the children and I went without. I was left to pick up the pieces, to make do, and to stretch every dollar just to keep food on the table. The emotional abandonment cut just as deeply as the physical abuse had before.

I couldn't do it alone. I had to build a plan—one that would allow me to leave safely without making him suspicious. The first step was identifying the resources I had around me—resources I had denied myself for so long: friends and professionals who could offer support. But even asking for help was terrifying. It meant admitting that I had been living in fear, acknowledging that I wasn't as strong as I had led myself to believe. I had to let go of my pride and the shame that had kept me silent. It was the hardest thing I had ever done, but in the end, it was the first real step toward freedom.

Creating a Safety Plan: Steps to Leave an Abusive Relationship Safely

Guide: Creating a Safety Plan

1. **Identify a Safe Place:** The first thing I did was figure out where I could go if I needed to leave quickly. While my options were limited, I had a few trusted friends who I knew would take me in if I had to escape in the middle of the night. I also researched shelters and support groups, just in case I had nowhere else to turn. It wasn't easy, but it gave me something to hold onto—a lifeline, even if I wasn't sure when I'd need it.

2. **Keep Important Documents Accessible:** I knew leaving would require organization, but I couldn't risk him finding out. So, I started secretly gathering important documents—my ID, birth certificate, bank information, and legal papers—and stored them in a safe place: a hidden drawer or a trusted friend's house. That way, if the time came, I could grab them quickly and leave without hesitation.

3. **Have a Bag Ready:** I packed a small, discreet bag with the essentials—clothes, toiletries, emergency cash, and a phone charger. It wasn't much, but it was enough to get me through the first few days. The goal was to make it portable and easy to grab without raising suspicion. If I needed to leave in a hurry, I wanted to be prepared.

4. **Create an Exit Strategy:** Planning the moment I would leave was critical. I had to observe his patterns—when he'd be away for work, when he'd be out with friends. I couldn't risk leaving when he was around. If I left during one of his outbursts, it could be dangerous. Timing was everything. Though I had a plan, I struggled to know when the "right" moment would come. That's when I had to trust my instincts and listen to that quiet, inner voice telling me it was time.

5. **Reach Out for Support:** I couldn't do it alone. I started confiding in a few trusted people—friends, family members, or therapists who understood what I was going through. I kept it discreet because I didn't want him to suspect anything, but I knew I needed support in case things went wrong. It felt incredibly vulnerable to ask for help, but each conversation made me feel stronger.

6. **Plan for Financial Independence:** One of my biggest fears was financial dependence. He controlled the money, and I had nothing of my own. In the months leading up to my decision to leave, I quietly set aside a small amount of money—hidden, of course—so I could buy the essentials once I left. I also researched financial support and legal aid available for women in abusive relationships. It was terrifying to think about living without money, but each small step gave me a sense of control over my future.

7. **Practice Escaping in a Safe Environment:** I knew that when the time came, I would need to act quickly. To prepare, I practiced my escape plan. I ran through the motions in my mind: grabbing the bag, getting to the car, and driving to a safe place. It might sound extreme, but it gave me a sense of empowerment. I wasn't waiting passively for the storm—I was preparing for the moment when I would take control of my life again.

8. **Know the Legal Options:** I made sure to understand my legal options. I researched how to obtain a Domestic Violence Order (DVO) and what the process entailed. I knew I had to prepare myself for the legal battle that might follow. Having this knowledge gave me confidence, knowing that the law would protect me once I took that first step.

The Fears That Almost Stopped Me

Despite all my planning, there were moments when fear nearly stopped me. What if he came home early and caught me? What if I made the wrong move and put myself in more danger? The unknowns were paralyzing. But the more I planned, the more I realized that staying was the real danger. I couldn't live in fear forever. I had to trust that God would guide my steps, even when I couldn't see the way clearly.

There were nights when fear kept me awake, and I doubted myself. Could I really do this? Could I really leave everything behind? But the voice of God in my heart reminded me that I wasn't alone. *"The Lord is my refuge and my strength, an ever-present help in trouble."* **(Psalm 46:1)** With each prayer and each step forward, I began to trust in His protection and His timing.

Leaving wasn't easy. It was messy. It was uncertain. But the more I prepared, the clearer it became: the storm would not last forever. I had to take that first step—however terrifying it was—and trust that God would meet me on the other side.

If you're in the midst of planning your own escape, take a moment to breathe. Know that you are stronger than you think. The fear, the obstacles, and the unknowns are real, but so is your courage. And you don't have to do this alone. Take one step at a time, and trust that with each step, you are moving toward freedom.

Study Spotlight: The Danger Period

"Dr. Jacquelyn Campbell's research warns that the first two weeks after leaving are the most dangerous for survivors. This is why careful safety planning is so critical. Leaving is courageous—but it also requires wisdom and protection. You are not paranoid; the danger is real, and planning is survival."

Source: Campbell, J. C. (2003). Risk factors for femicide in abusive relationships: Results from a multisite case control study. American Journal of Public Health, 93(7), 1089-1097.

A Letter to You

I know what it's like to get lost in the illusion of a perfect beginning—to believe you've found the love of your life, only to be blindsided by manipulation and control. If you're reading this and wondering whether you're in a relationship where the love feels too intense, too perfect, or even too controlling, I want you to hear this loud and clear: You are not crazy. You are not weak. You are not unworthy of real love.

God created you to be cherished, valued, and to live a life filled with peace. He never intended for you to live in fear, to feel like you must earn love through sacrifice or pain. The love you deserve is one that uplifts you, one that makes you feel seen, heard, and safe.

If you find yourself questioning the foundation of your relationship, take a step back. Listen to your heart. Listen to your faith. Listen to that quiet voice inside telling you something isn't right. You are worthy of peace, and you are worthy of a love free from manipulation and fear.

Start by holding onto this truth: You deserve to be loved for who you are, not for what you can give. And remember, God is with you every step of the way, guiding you toward the life and love you were always meant to have.

Dawn Williams

JOURNAL PROMPT:
Reflection

1. What steps do you need to take (or did you take) to prepare for your freedom? Who can you trust to help you?

My Thoughts :

_____
_____
_____
_____
_____
_____
_____

Affirmation: I am capable of making wise choices. I deserve to live in peace and safety.

Prayer: God, I ask for protection and wisdom as I prepare to step into freedom. Lead me to the right people and resources Be my shield and my guide. Amen.

the REBUILT WOMAN

Stage 2: The Breaking Point – Finding the Courage to Leave

CHAPTER 7
The Aftermath: The Reality of Leaving

I left him, but I didn't leave unscathed. There was relief in walking away, a sense of freedom I hadn't known in years. Yet, that relief wasn't immediate—it was tangled with grief, emotional exhaustion, and the disorienting weight of everything I had experienced. I had imagined that once I was out, the healing would be simple, that I could just start over and everything would fall into place. But life, I soon realized, wasn't that easy.

The emotional whiplash hit me first. Relief mixed with guilt, freedom wrapped in fear. I could breathe again, but the weight of everything I'd been through didn't lift just because I walked out the door.

The past continued to haunt me—memories, thought patterns, and doubts about my own worth. I felt as though I had been ripped open, raw and exposed, with nothing left but the need to rebuild.

I had the relief of no longer living in fear, but there were moments when the silence of my new life felt like an echo of my pain. It wasn't the peace I had imagined, but something far more complex—a mix of grief and freedom, loss and hope.

The Aftermath: The Reality of Leaving

The Grief of Loss

The grief hit hardest in the quiet moments. When I looked at the empty spaces in my life—the vacant bed, the empty house—it was as though I was grieving the life I had dreamed of. I had invested so much of myself into that relationship. I had hoped that the love I offered could fix things, that somehow, things would get better. But now, I was grieving not just the person I thought he was, but also the person I had become in his presence. I had lost a part of myself in that relationship, a part I wasn't sure I could ever get back.

It was hard to let go of the dreams I had, the idea that we could be a family that the pain would one day fade into something beautiful. But I had to remind myself that those dreams were based on illusions. The reality was that I had been surviving, not truly living. I was not meant to lose myself in the process of loving someone else.

Relief, But Not Freedom

Relief was there, but it came in waves, always followed by moments of doubt. I had the freedom I longed for, but it wasn't the kind of freedom I had expected. I had been so accustomed to living in fear, to seeking validation in all the wrong places, that it took time to adjust to my new reality. There were moments when the weight of everything I had experienced felt too much to bear. I was alone now, but I wasn't truly alone. I had God with me.

The most unexpected struggle was the loneliness. After years of being isolated, both physically and emotionally, I was now on my own. The support network I had once relied on was fractured, and rebuilding those connections felt like an uphill battle. But as I prayed and sought God's guidance, I realized He had never truly left me. In fact, He had been waiting for me to turn to Him, to lean into His strength rather than relying on my own.

The Aftermath: The Reality of Leaving

Faith and Spiritual Healing

In the aftermath, my faith became the foundation of my healing. I leaned into God's promises, especially in the darkest moments when everything seemed too heavy to bear. *"The Lord is close to the brokenhearted and saves those who are crushed in spirit."* **(Psalm 34:18)** I clung to that truth. I realized that God was near in my brokenness, and that my journey of healing was not just about escaping the past but learning to trust Him with my future.

I prayed more than I ever had before. It wasn't always beautiful or eloquent, but it was raw and real. I asked God to heal my wounds, to help me rebuild, and to remind me of my worth. Slowly, through those prayers, I began to feel His presence in new ways. I knew I wasn't alone in this. He was with me every step of the way, even in my doubt, even in my pain.

Healing wasn't just about leaving; it was about learning to live again, learning to trust in God's plan for my life. It was about allowing Him to heal the emotional scars that no one else could see and trusting that my brokenness could be made beautiful in His hands.

Psychological Healing

Amidst my spiritual healing, I knew I needed psychological healing as well. The damage done to my mind—years of manipulation, gaslighting, and emotional abuse—didn't simply vanish with his absence. I found myself questioning everything: my choices, my judgment, my worth. I had been conditioned to believe that I wasn't enough, that I couldn't do anything without his approval.

But through therapy and self-reflection, I began to unravel the lies I had believed about myself. I learned to identify the toxic thought patterns that had kept me trapped in the cycle of abuse. I had to relearn how to trust myself and make decisions without second-guessing everything. It was difficult, and it took time, but I began to realize that the trauma I had endured did not define me.

The Aftermath: The Reality of Leaving

I also had to learn to forgive—not just him, but myself. The guilt I carried for staying, for allowing things to continue for so long, weighed heavily on me. But I came to understand that forgiveness wasn't about excusing the hurt; it was about releasing myself from the chains of regret. I had done the best I could with the knowledge I had at the time. And now, I was choosing to move forward, free from the shame that had held me captive for so long.

Navigating Post-Separation Abuse

Even after leaving, the abuse didn't stop—it simply took on a different form. The emotional manipulation continued, but now it was through flaunting his reckless lifestyle, parading younger women in front of me, and making sure I saw how "happy" he was without me. He surrounded himself with addicts, criminals, and people who thrived on chaos, bringing drama into my life and my children's lives, even though we were no longer together. It wasn't just the pain of separation; it was the ongoing torment of knowing he was intentionally trying to hurt me in new ways.

There were nights when I'd receive messages from him, laced with both anger and seduction, as if he were testing whether he still had control over me. He'd disappear from the kids' lives for weeks, only to return with extravagant gifts, acting like the fun parent while I was left to clean up the emotional mess. The manipulation was relentless. "No one else would want you," he would say, as if I was still tethered to him, as if my freedom was just an illusion.

One of the hardest realizations was that leaving him didn't mean escaping the toxicity. His choices continued to affect me, from the people he allowed into his life to the reckless way he handled himself. Drugs, violence toward the children, and irresponsibility—his downward spiral didn't just hurt him; it spilled over into my world, forcing me to shield my children from it. I had to stand my ground, set boundaries, and refuse to let his self-destruction pull me back in. Some days, it felt like I was still trapped in his storm, but the difference was—I now had the strength to fight back.

The Aftermath: The Reality of Leaving

Legal Steps and Emotional Recovery

After another violent altercation, during which he was experiencing psychosis from drug abuse, I took steps to protect myself and the children legally. I knew I needed to establish boundaries and ensure he couldn't hurt us again. I called the police, and they advised me to apply for a Domestic Violence Order (DVO), which helped establish clear legal consequences if he tried to contact or threaten me or the children again. While it provided a sense of protection, it was also draining. The legal process often felt like reliving the trauma, speaking about things I wanted to forget. I had to face my past head-on, and that was difficult. There were moments when I felt hopeless, unsure if I could keep going, unsure if I was strong enough to keep fighting. But I reminded myself that healing was a journey, not a destination. It would take time. I had to be patient with myself, even when it felt like I was taking two steps forward and one step back.

I sought comfort from close friends and support groups, anything to help me rebuild the shattered parts of myself. I leaned on my faith more than ever during this time. God was my refuge when everything felt too much to handle. *"The Lord is near to the brokenhearted and saves the crushed in spirit."* **(Psalm 34:18)** His love was constant and I clung to that truth when everything else felt uncertain.

In moments of despair, I would remind myself that healing wasn't linear. Some days were better than others, but even on the bad days, I was still moving forward. Every tear, every prayer, every step of faith was part of my process of recovery.

Legal Steps and Emotional Recovery

The reality of leaving an abusive relationship is that healing doesn't happen all at once. It comes in waves—some days, you feel strong and free; other days, the weight of everything hits you again. But through it all, I have learned to trust God's process. He is with me every step of the way, offering grace when I falter, strength when I feel weak, and love when I feel unworthy.

The Aftermath: The Reality of Leaving

I still struggle, of course. There are days when the pain resurfaces, when I feel the weight of all I have lost. But I've come to understand that healing is not a straight line—it's a journey. And with God's help, I am walking that journey one day at a time. If you are in the aftermath of leaving, remember that you are not alone. Healing takes time, but it is possible. You are worthy of love, peace, and a future where you can thrive. Lean on your faith, trust in God's timing, and allow yourself the grace to heal. Your story is not over—it is just beginning.

Study Spotlight: Financial Abuse

"A study by Adams and colleagues found that 99% of survivors experience financial abuse. Whether through controlling money, sabotaging work, or creating dependence, finances often become another chain. If you struggled with money after leaving, it's not a personal failure—it's a common tactic abusers use to maintain power."

Source: Adams, A. E., Sullivan, C. M., Bybee, D., & Greeson, M. R. (2008). Development of the scale of economic abuse. Violence Against Women, 14(5), 563–588.

A Letter to You

I know what it's like to get lost in the illusion of a perfect beginning—to believe you've found the love of your life, only to be blindsided by manipulation and control. If you're reading this and wondering whether you're in a relationship where the love feels too intense, too perfect, or even too controlling, I want you to hear this loud and clear: You are not crazy. You are not weak. You are not unworthy of real love.

God created you to be cherished, valued, and to live a life filled with peace. He never intended for you to live in fear, to feel like you must earn love through sacrifice or pain. The love you deserve is one that uplifts you, one that makes you feel seen, heard, and safe.

If you find yourself questioning the foundation of your relationship, take a step back. Listen to your heart. Listen to your faith. Listen to that quiet voice inside telling you something isn't right. You are worthy of peace, and you are worthy of a love free from manipulation and fear.

Start by holding onto this truth: You deserve to be loved for who you are, not for what you can give. And remember, God is with you every step of the way, guiding you toward the life and love you were always meant to have.

Dawn Williams

JOURNAL PROMPT:

Reflection

1. How did you feel in the days and weeks after leaving? What emotions surprised you?

My Thoughts :

_____
_____
_____
_____
_____
_____
_____
_____
_____

Affirmation: Healing is not linear. Every step forward, no matter how small, is still progress.

Prayer: Lord, the road ahead feels overwhelming. Remind me that I am not alone. Give me patience with myself as I grieve, heal, and rebuild. Amen

THE REBUILT WOMAN

Stage 3: The Rebuilding – Healing & Rediscovering Yourself

Rebuilding after abuse is not just about leaving the past behind; it's about **learning to live fully again**—in wholeness, freedom, and truth. The wounds left by trauma go beyond visible scars; they affect our **mind, body, spirit, and relationships**. This is why true healing must be holistic, addressing each part of our being.

For years, you may have lived in survival mode—navigating fear, pain, and confusion. Now, as you step into this next stage, you are invited into something deeper: **a process of renewal**. You are not just recovering from the past; you are rediscovering who God created you to be.

This journey of rebuilding aligns with my **Theory of 4-Dimensional Healing**—each representing an essential part of your restoration:

1. Healing the Mind – Renewing Thought Patterns Trauma rewires the brain, often leading to negative self-beliefs, anxiety, and emotional triggers. Your mind has been shaped by years of survival, but healing requires **renewing your thoughts** (Romans 12:2). In this stage, you will learn how to:

- Identify and challenge negative self-talk
- Rewire thought patterns shaped by trauma
- Develop emotional resilience and self-compassion

2. Healing the Body – Releasing Stored Trauma Your body has carried the weight of your experiences—sometimes manifesting as chronic pain, fatigue, or autoimmune conditions. Scientific research confirms what the Bible has always taught: our bodies store trauma. The good news is that healing is possible. This section will guide you in:
- Reconnecting with your body through movement and self-care
- Understanding how stress and trauma impact the nervous system
- Nourishing your body in a way that promotes healing

3. Healing the Spirit – Restoring Faith and Identity Abuse often distorts our sense of self-worth and our view of God. You may have felt abandoned, unworthy, or unloved. But God has never left you. He is inviting you to reclaim your identity as His beloved daughter. This section will help you: ·Rebuild trust in God and in His plan for your life
- Let go of shame and embrace grace
- Deepen your spiritual connection through prayer, worship, and scripture

4. Healing in Community – Finding Safe, Supportive Relationships Trauma isolates, but healing happens in connection. Many women struggle with trust after abuse, but **you were never meant to heal alone.** The Rebuilt Woman healing circles were founded in 2019 with just two women, bravely sharing their raw and real stories. That small group became a place of **support, accountability, and transformation**—a model of what is possible when we heal together. As you move forward, you will learn how to:
- Build safe, healthy relationships
- Break free from dysfunctional patterns
- Surround yourself with a Christ-centered community

A Prayer for Renewal: Heavenly Father, I give You every part of me—my mind, my body, my spirit, and my relationships. I ask You to heal me completely and lead me toward the life You have prepared for me. Fill me with Your truth, peace, and strength as I rebuild. I trust You, Lord, and I choose to walk forward in faith. In Jesus' name, Amen.

the REBUILT WOMAN

Stage 3: The Rebuilding – Healing & Rediscovering Yourself

CHAPTER 8
Facing the Trauma

When I left, I thought I was leaving everything behind—the fear, the pain, the abuse. But what I didn't realize was that the trauma would follow me. It wasn't just in the memories; it was in my body, my thoughts, my reactions. I had survived, but I had also been scarred in ways I couldn't yet understand.

The first thing I noticed was how difficult it was to settle into the quiet. I had spent so many years in survival mode, always bracing for the next blow, always ready to flee, freeze, or fight. But now, I had nothing to fight, no one to flee from, and nothing to freeze in response to. Still, my body reacted as though I were in danger—trapped in that cycle of abuse—even when I was safe. I would startle at the sound of a door slamming, my heart would race when someone raised their voice, or I would flinch when someone reached out to touch me. I didn't feel safe in my own skin.

The trauma had left its mark, and healing wasn't as simple as just walking away. The damage was deep—embedded in my psyche and spirit. I felt like I was carrying the weight of years of fear, shame, and guilt, as if it were all part of me, as though I couldn't separate who I was from the trauma I had experienced. I questioned myself constantly: *Why didn't I leave sooner? Why did I let it go on for so long? What did I do wrong?*

The Aftermath: The Reality of Leaving

The Struggle with Guilt and Shame

One of the hardest things to confront was the guilt and shame I carried. I felt guilty for not leaving sooner, for not protecting myself or my children better, for allowing him to control me for so long. I thought about the warning signs I had ignored, the times I let my intuition be silenced by love or fear.

I also felt ashamed of how I had allowed myself to be manipulated, how I had believed his lies. I wondered if I was weak, if I was somehow less-than for staying. The shame was overwhelming, and it kept me from fully embracing the healing process. I was ashamed of how long it took me to leave, ashamed of the times I had excused his behavior, ashamed of the person I had become in that relationship.

But over time, I began to realize that guilt and shame do not come from God. They are tools of the enemy to keep us trapped in our pain and self-doubt. "There is therefore now no condemnation for those who are in Christ Jesus." (Romans 8:1) I had to remind myself of this truth every day. God's love wasn't conditional on my perfection or my decisions. His love was constant, even in my brokenness.

Understanding Trauma Responses

The trauma I experienced wasn't just emotional—it was physiological. My body had been trained to react in ways that kept me alive in a dangerous environment. Fight, flight, freeze, and fawn—these are the survival mechanisms we use when we're under threat, and they became my default responses to stress.

- **Fight:** There were times when I fought back, whether with words or actions. I would argue, shout, or become defensive, as if preparing for an attack. But it wasn't just self-defense—it was a learned behavior, an automatic response to being constantly on edge.

- **Flight:** Other times, I would shut down emotionally and distance myself. I would avoid confrontation or retreat into myself, both physically and emotionally. It was my way of escaping the tension, even if it meant sacrificing my own voice.

The Aftermath: The Reality of Leaving

- **Freeze:** There were moments when I simply froze—paralyzed by fear or confusion, unsure how to react or what was happening. It was as though my body couldn't move or respond, even though my mind screamed for action.

- **Fawn:** At times, I became hyper-vigilant, trying to please him, anticipating his needs or moods. I would go along with whatever he wanted, just to keep the peace, just to avoid another outburst. This is known as people-pleasing, and it stems from a deep need for approval, especially from an abuser.

These responses were deeply ingrained in me, and they didn't disappear when I left. They continued to shape how I reacted to stress, new relationships, and even to myself. But understanding these trauma responses was the first step in breaking free from them. I had to retrain my body and mind, learning how to respond differently to the triggers that still lingered

Understanding the effects on your body

The Red Zone and Blue Zone are terms often used to describe different responses to stress and trauma, particularly in relation to the nervous system. These zones align with the fight, flight, freeze, and fawn responses—automatic survival reactions from the body.

Red Zone (Hyperarousal) The Red Zone represents a state of hyperarousal, where the body is in high alert due to stress or danger. It is linked to the sympathetic nervous system (fight-or- flight response). In this state, emotions and behaviors may include:
- Anger, rage, aggression (fight)
- Panic, anxiety, restlessness (flight)
- Irritability, impulsivity, emotional outbursts
- Rapid heartbeat, shallow breathing, muscle tension

This response often occurs when a person feels threatened or cornered, leading them to either attack the perceived threat (fight) or try to escape (flight).

The Aftermath: The Reality of Leaving

Blue Zone (Hypoarousal)

The Blue Zone represents a state of hypoarousal, where the nervous system shuts down due to overwhelm or prolonged stress. This is linked to the parasympathetic nervous system, specifically the dorsal vagal shutdown (freeze or fawn response). Symptoms include:
- ·Emotional numbness, disconnection, exhaustion
- ·Feeling empty, hopeless, or dissociated
- ·Slowed movement, difficulty speaking, brain fog
- ·Shutting down socially or withdrawing from others

The freeze response can make someone feel paralyzed or "stuck" in an abusive situation, while the fawn response can lead to people-pleasing and compliance to avoid conflict.

Understanding Your Stress Zone

Many survivors of trauma cycle between the **Red and Blue Zones,** struggling to find the **Green Zone**—a state of **balance, safety, and connection** where healing can take place. Recognizing these zones can help individuals understand their emotional responses and develop healthier ways to self-regulate.

Red and Blue Zones in My Story

For years, I lived between the **Red Zone and the Blue Zone**, cycling through survival responses without even realizing it. My body had learned to **adapt to the chaos,** constantly adjusting to the unpredictable storms of my relationship. When the tension would rise, when his voice sharpened, when his mood darkened —I would **instantly enter the Red Zone.** My heart would race, my body would tense, and my mind would scan for escape routes. **Would he lash out? Would he disappear? Would I need to calm him down, or should I stay silent and invisible?** The anxiety of never knowing kept my body on high alert. I became an expert at **reading his face, his footsteps, his energy**—anything to **predict the storm before it arrived.**

The Aftermath: The Reality of Leaving

But once the explosion passed, I would crash into the **Blue Zone**—numb, exhausted, **completely drained**. I would withdraw, dissociate, and go through the motions of daily life like a ghost. The silence after the storm was just as painful as the violence itself. He would disappear for days, **leaving me alone with the kids, ignoring us**, neglecting us. But in some ways, I almost preferred it. At least in his absence, I wasn't bracing for impact.

I convinced myself that if I could just stay small, stay quiet, keep the peace, maybe things would change. This was the fawn response—pleasing, adapting, making myself easy to love in hopes that he would finally love me back. But deep down, I was losing myself. My body never felt safe. My nervous system was always caught between fight, flight, freeze, and fawn, never finding true rest.

Breaking the Cycle and Finding the Green Zone

Healing meant recognizing that this cycle wasn't love—it was trauma. It meant understanding that when the nervous system is trapped in survival mode for too long, it starts to believe that chaos is normal, and peace becomes unfamiliar, even unsettling.

The first step was awareness—learning that my body wasn't broken; it had just been in survival mode for too long. I had to retrain myself to recognize safety, to create stability, and to calm my nervous system so I could think clearly and make decisions that weren't just about surviving, but about truly living.

The Aftermath: The Reality of Leaving

Healing from Trauma Responses

Healing from trauma is not a linear process. Some days, the responses would overwhelm me, and I'd feel as though I were back in that toxic environment, even though I was physically safe. But with each passing day, I grew stronger. I began to recognize my triggers, to pause before reacting, and to choose healthier ways of responding.

I sought therapy to help me process the trauma and understand how these responses were affecting my relationships and mental health. It wasn't easy to face the truth of what had happened, but with time, I learned how to sit with my pain without letting it define me.

I also turned to my faith. I spent hours in prayer, asking God to heal the scars that no one else could see. *"He heals the brokenhearted and binds up their wounds."* **(Psalm 147:3)** I leaned into His love and grace, knowing that I didn't have to carry this burden alone. I learned to surrender my fears, guilt, and shame to Him, and in doing so, I began to experience a deep peace I had never known before.

Psychological Healing and Rediscovering Yourself

Psychologically, I had to completely renew my mind, emotions, and address toxic behaviors through evidence-based therapies like CPT and CBT. I had to learn how to trust myself again. I had spent so long doubting my judgment, second-guessing my decisions, and living in a constant state of anxiety. I had to rebuild my sense of self-worth and rediscover who I was outside of the trauma.

It wasn't easy, and it didn't happen overnight. But with therapy, self-care, and spiritual healing, I began to see myself as more than just a survivor. I was a woman of strength, resilience, and someone who had been through the fire and emerged stronger on the other side.

The Aftermath: The Reality of Leaving

Study Spotlight: PTSD in Survivors

"Research shows that between 31% and 84% of survivors of domestic violence meet the criteria for PTSD—higher rates than some combat veterans. If you have flashbacks, nightmares, or hypervigilance, it isn't weakness. It's your body remembering the trauma. With help, healing is possible."

Source: Golding, J. M. (1999). Intimate partner violence as a risk factor for mental disorders: A meta-analysis. Journal of Family Violence, 14(2), 99–132.

A Letter to You

If you are walking through trauma recovery, know that healing is possible. You are not defined by what happened to you. While trauma may shape you, it does not have to control you. With time, faith, and the support you need, you will rediscover who you are and rebuild your life. Remember, God is with you every step of the way. He will restore what the enemy has stolen and make you whole again. Trust His timing, lean into His grace, and know that you are worthy of healing.

Dawn Williams

JOURNAL PROMPT:
Reflection

1. How has your trauma shaped the way you see yourself, others, and God? What lies has it told you?

My Thoughts

_____
_____
_____
_____
_____
_____
_____
_____
_____
_____
_____
_____

Affirmation: ··My trauma does not define me. I am healing, and will not carry shame that does not belong to me.

Prayer: ··God, help me to process my pain without being consumed by it. Show me the truth about who I am in You. Amen.

the REBUILT WOMAN

Stage 3: The Rebuilding – Healing & Rediscovering Yourself

CHAPTER 9
The Silent Wounds: How Trauma Affects the Mind, Body, and Spirit

The Day My Body Gave In

I will never forget the morning I woke up and couldn't move from the waist down. Panic surged through me as I tried to sit up, but my legs wouldn't respond. My body—this body that had carried four children and endured years of stress, pain, and survival—had suddenly shut down.

Rushed to the hospital, I underwent test after test. Then came the diagnosis: sarcoidosis, a rare autoimmune disease. They told me it was incurable, that my body was attacking itself, and that I would have to manage it for the rest of my life.

I should have been devastated, but strangely, I wasn't. I refused to accept that my body was beyond repair. Deep down, something in me knew that this disease wasn't just physical. It was the culmination of years of stress, fear, trauma, and suppression. My body had been carrying wounds that my heart and mind hadn't fully acknowledged.

In that moment, I knew I had a choice: to accept this diagnosis as my permanent reality, or to seek healing—physically, emotionally, and spiritually. I chose healing.

The Silent Wounds: How Trauma Affects the Mind, Body, and Spirit
When Trauma Lives in the Body

For years, I pushed through life, carrying stress like a badge of honor. I lived in survival mode, always waiting for the next explosion, the next betrayal, the next disappointment. I didn't realize that trauma wasn't just in my mind—it had seeped into every cell of my body.

Trauma changes us. It rewires the brain, disrupts the nervous system, and even alters the immune system. This is why so many survivors of abuse and long-term stress develop **chronic illnesses, autoimmune disorders, anxiety, depression, and even chronic pain**. The body carries what the heart and mind try to ignore.

What I experienced—losing the ability to walk—was the body's way of saying: Enough.

The Body Remembers: Trauma's Impact on the Mind and Body

I will never forget the day my body completely shut down. I woke up unable to move from the waist down, terrified and confused. At the hospital, I was diagnosed with sarcoidosis, an autoimmune disease. The doctors told me it was incurable, but something in me refused to accept that. As a mother of four young children, I couldn't afford to stay sick. I turned to God, prayer, and radical life changes.

Over the next two years, as I surrendered my pain and trauma, I saw my health slowly restore. When I went back for blood tests, the disease had completely disappeared—no medical explanation, just divine healing and a transformed life. At the time, I didn't fully understand how deeply trauma was affecting my body. But now, I see the connection so clearly. Studies have shown that trauma is not just an emotional wound—it is stored in the body, rewiring the nervous system and affecting the immune system, mental health, and even physical mobility. In *The Body Keeps the Score,* psychiatrist Dr. Bessel van der Kolk explains how unprocessed trauma leads to chronic stress, inflammation, and disease, often manifesting in autoimmune disorders, digestive issues, and even chronic pain.

The Silent Wounds: How Trauma Affects the Mind, Body, and Spirit

When we live in constant survival mode, our bodies are flooded with stress hormones like cortisol and adrenaline, weakening our immune system and keeping us in a state of hypervigilance. This is why so many trauma survivors struggle with chronic illness, anxiety, depression, and exhaustion—our bodies carry what our minds try to forget.

The Body Keeps Score

Science backs up what I went through. When you live under prolonged stress and trauma:
- Your nervous system stays in a constant state of fight-or-flight.
- Your immune system weakens, making you susceptible to illnesses.
- Your hormones get thrown out of balance, leading to fatigue, brain fog, and weight changes.
- Your muscles and joints tense up, leading to chronic pain and inflammation.

The body remembers what the mind forgets. And until we address the emotional wounds, the body will keep speaking—through illness, pain, and exhaustion.

Breaking the Cycle: How I Found Healing

When the doctors told me my disease was incurable, I turned to the only place I knew had the final say—God.

I prayed like I had never prayed before. I surrendered my body, my pain, and my fear at His feet. But I didn't just pray—I listened. And I felt God lead me on a journey of healing that went beyond just my physical body.

Over the next two years, I changed my life:
- I released stress and unforgiveness. I stopped holding onto bitterness and allowed myself to heal emotionally.
- I changed my habits. I adjusted my diet, rested, and honored my body instead of pushing it past its limits.

The Silent Wounds: How Trauma Affects the Mind, Body, and Spirit

- I surrounded myself with faith and support. I sought out prayer, community, and healing spaces that uplifted me.
- I began speaking life over myself. I stopped saying, "I am sick," and started declaring, "I am healed."

And one day, the healing was complete. I returned for blood tests, and the disease was gone. No sign of it in my body. The doctors couldn't explain it, but I knew—I had experienced a miracle. Not just of physical healing, but of mind, body, and spirit restoration.

What This Means for You

If you've experienced trauma, your body may be carrying the weight of it—even if you don't realize it yet. You may feel exhausted all the time, develop unexplained health issues, or struggle with constant anxiety. But you are not broken. Healing is possible.

Here's what I want you to know:

1. Your body is not your enemy. It's trying to protect you, even when it's in pain.
2. Healing takes time, but it is possible. Just as trauma rewires the brain and body, healing can, too.
3. God is your healer. He doesn't just want to save your soul—He wants to restore every part of you.

Steps to Begin Your Healing

1. Acknowledge what your body is saying. Are you always tired? Do you get sick often? Listen to the signs.
2. Prioritize rest and nourishment. Reduce stress, eat well, and allow yourself to slow down.
3. Find a safe space to heal. Trauma healing happens in community. Consider joining a Rebuilt Woman Healing Circle (details at the back of this book).
4. Pray for healing, but also take action. Faith and works go hand in hand. Seek therapy, counseling, or support groups if needed.
5. Speak life over yourself. Declare that you are healing, you are whole, and your past does not define your future.

The Silent Wounds: How Trauma Affects the Mind, Body, and Spirit

Self-Reflection & Journal Questions

1. In what ways has your body been speaking to you? Have you noticed any physical symptoms of stress or trauma?
2. How have you been coping with emotional pain? Are there habits or thoughts that may be harming you instead of healing you?
3. What steps can you take today to begin caring for your body and mind in a healthier way?
4. Have you ever considered that God wants to heal you not just spiritually, but physically and emotionally, too? What does that mean for you?
5. How can you start speaking life and healing over yourself instead of accepting pain and brokenness as your identity?

A Prayer for Healing

Father God, I come before You today, bringing all my pain, fears, and burdens. You see every wound, every scar, and every broken place within me. I have carried this pain for so long, and I no longer want to live in survival mode.

Lord, I ask You to heal my body, mind, and spirit. I surrender the stress, the trauma, and the weight of the past. Show me how to care for my body as a temple of Your Holy Spirit. Help me release bitterness, fear, and anxiety, replacing them with peace, strength, and wholeness.

I declare today that I am not defined by what has happened to me—I am defined by who You say I am. I am loved. I am chosen. I am healed. I receive Your healing power and trust You to restore every part of me.

In Jesus' Name, Amen.

You Are Not Meant to Live in Survival Mode

I want you to know that you were not created to live in a constant state of fear, exhaustion, or pain. Trauma may have left its mark on you, but it does not get to write your story.

I am living proof that God restores, that the body can heal, and that trauma does not have to define you. And if He did it for me, He can do it for you, too. It's time to begin your journey back to wholeness. Are you ready?

A Letter to You

If you are walking through trauma recovery, know that healing is possible. You are not defined by what happened to you. While trauma may shape you, it does not have to control you. With time, faith, and the support you need, you will rediscover who you are and rebuild your life. Remember, God is with you every step of the way. He will restore what the enemy has stolen and make you whole again. Trust His timing, lean into His grace, and know that you are worthy of healing.

Dawn Williams

JOURNAL PROMPT:
Reflection

1. Have you ever experienced physical symptoms (such as chronic pain, headaches, or fatigue) that seemed to have no medical explanation?
2. How do you respond to stress? Does it manifest in your body through tension, stomach issues, or other symptoms?
3. What steps can you take to prioritize both emotional and physical healing?

My Thoughts

_____
_____
_____
_____
_____
_____
_____
_____
_____
_____
_____
_____
_____

Prayer: Father, I invite You into the deepest parts of my pain. I surrender the trauma my body has carried for so long. Heal me—physically, emotionally, and spiritually. Teach me to release what no longer serves me and embrace the peace You have for me. I trust You with my healing.
In Jesus' name, Amen.

THE REBUILT WOMAN

the REBUILT WOMAN

Stage 3: The Rebuilding – Healing & Rediscovering Yourself

CHAPTER 10
Renew My Power

There were days when I didn't feel like myself. When I looked in the mirror, I saw a woman who had been broken, silenced, and made to feel small. But deep inside, I knew that woman wasn't me. I had been through the fire, and I was ready to rise. Yet, the journey to reclaiming my power wasn't instantaneous—it was a process, one small but powerful step at a time.

At first, those steps felt insignificant, almost meaningless. But as I kept moving forward, I began to feel something shift. It wasn't a dramatic change, but it was real. My confidence, my self-worth, my sense of power started to return. And it all began with one simple decision: to choose myself.

The First Step: Reclaiming My Self-Worth

I started by making a commitment to honor myself. For so long, I had allowed my identity to be shaped by the opinions and actions of others—by the abuse, manipulation, and lies. But I was no longer willing to let my past dictate my future. I was determined to reclaim my worth, to see myself as God saw me—not as someone broken, but as someone loved, chosen, and worthy of respect.

Renew My Power

Each day, I began with a prayer, reminding myself that I was a child of God, loved and valued beyond measure. "I am fearfully and wonderfully made" (Psalm 139:14). This truth became my anchor. I repeated it over and over until I truly believed it again. I let go of the shame, guilt, and negative self-talk that had plagued me for so long. In its place, I embraced the truth of who I was in Christ.

The Power of Boundaries

The next step in rebuilding my confidence was learning how to set boundaries. For too long, I had ignored my own needs, trying to keep the peace and make everyone else happy. But I learned that boundaries aren't just about saying "no" to others; they're about saying "yes" to myself.

I began by recognizing what was draining me—emotionally, physically, and spiritually. I realized I had to protect my energy, my peace, and my mental health. So, I started setting boundaries with people, places, and situations that no longer served me. I said "no" to toxic relationships, to people who didn't respect my worth, and to circumstances that pulled me back into old patterns.

Setting boundaries wasn't always easy, nor was it always comfortable. But I discovered that setting boundaries was an act of self-love. It was a declaration that I was worthy of respect, deserving of kindness and honor. And every time I enforced a boundary, I felt a little stronger, a little more powerful.

Affirmations & Declarations

Along with setting boundaries, I began declaring truths over my life every day. These affirmations became my spiritual and emotional toolkit—powerful words that helped me fight against the lies and self-doubt.
- "I am worthy of love and respect."
- "I am enough, just as I am."
- "I am strong, resilient, and capable of overcoming any challenge."
- "God has a good plan for my life, and I trust His timing."
- "I am not defined by my past; I am shaped by my faith and my future."

Renew My Power

I would say these declarations out loud in front of the mirror, sometimes with tears in my eyes, but always with faith in my heart. Over time, I began to feel the truth of those words settle deep within my soul. I wasn't just saying them—I was believing them. I was becoming them.

The Importance of Self-Care

Healing also meant taking care of myself. I had spent so much of my life giving to others, neglecting my own needs in the process. But now, I realized that I had to prioritize my own well-being. Self-care wasn't selfish—it was necessary.

I began by taking small steps to nurture myself. I took walks in nature to clear my mind and connect with God. I set aside time for prayer and meditation, creating space to hear God's voice and find peace. I allowed myself moments of rest, understanding that healing didn't mean doing everything at once. It meant taking it one step at a time.

I also began taking better care of my body. I reestablished healthy routines, like eating well and exercising. I treated myself with kindness—both physically and emotionally—recognizing that my body had carried so much pain and deserved to be treated with love and respect.

Spiritual Renewal

Along with these practical steps, my faith was central to renewing my strength. I turned to God's word, finding comfort in scriptures that affirmed my worth, my strength, and my purpose. "For I know the plans I have for you," declares the Lord, "plans to prosper you and not to harm you, plans to give you a hope and a future." (Jeremiah 29:11) These words became a lifeline, reminding me that God's plans for me were good—even in moments of pain. I also sought healing through prayer, asking God to renew my strength, restore what had been lost, and help me see myself the way He sees me. I prayed for the courage to break free from old patterns and step into the new life He had for me.

Renew My Power

Taking Small Steps Toward Confidence

Rebuilding my confidence didn't happen overnight, but I began to see progress. Each step—no matter how small—was a victory. Every prayer, affirmation, and boundary I set brought me closer to reclaiming my power.

But it wasn't just about rebuilding confidence. It was about rediscovering who I am in Christ—who I've always been, before the abuse, before the pain, before the lies. I was reminded that I am God's masterpiece, fearfully and wonderfully made, and nothing that happened to me could ever change that truth.

The Power of Moving Forward

If you're reading this and wondering if you'll ever feel confident again, let me tell you this: You will. You are not defined by what happened to you. You are not defined by the trauma, the guilt, or the shame. You are defined by who you are in Christ—strong, loved, and worthy of peace and joy.

Take those small steps, one day at a time. Start with the truth of who you are, and let that truth guide you forward. Set boundaries, speak affirmations, prioritize self-care, and lean into God's love. You have the power to rebuild your confidence, renew your strength, and reclaim the life you were meant to live.

Remember, you are not alone. You are powerful, and with God's help, you will rise again.

A Letter to You

If you are walking through trauma recovery, know that healing is possible. You are not defined by what happened to you. While trauma may shape you, it does not have to control you. With time, faith, and the support you need, you will rediscover who you are and rebuild your life. Remember, God is with you every step of the way. He will restore what the enemy has stolen and make you whole again. Trust His timing, lean into His grace, and know that you are worthy of healing.

Dawn Williams

JOURNAL PROMPT:
Reflection

1. List three small victories you've had in your healing journey. How can you continue to build on them?

My Thoughts:

_____
_____
_____
_____
_____
_____
_____
_____

Affirmation: Each day, I grow stronger. My past does not control my future.

Prayer: Lord, renew my spirit and restore my confidence. Remind me that I am fearfully and wonderfully made, worthy of love and respect. Amen.

the REBUILT WOMAN

Stage 4: The Transformation – A New Beginning

There comes a moment in your healing journey when you look back and realize—you are no longer the person who once lived in survival mode. The pain that once defined you has lost its grip, and in its place, something new is emerging: purpose. Healing isn't just about overcoming the past; it's about stepping into the fullness of who God created you to be.

This stage is about transformation, not just recovery. It's about taking all that you've learned, all that you've healed from, and using it to build a life of meaning. You're no longer just surviving—you're stepping into a future filled with intention, faith, and purpose. This is where you discover that **you were never meant to walk this journey alone.**

Healing happens in community. Jesus Himself modeled this—He didn't walk alone but surrounded Himself with a small, trusted group. The Bible reminds us, *"For where two or three gather in my name, there am I with them"* **(Matthew 18:20). Finding your healing circle—two or more people who truly see you, support you, and hold you accountable—is essential in this stage.** Transformation happens when we are seen, known, and encouraged to keep growing.

I know this because I've lived it. There was a time when I felt like I wouldn't make it through. The weight of pain, grief, and confusion was too much to bear on my own. But God sent me **one friend**. A circle of two. She was compassionate, empathetic, and—most importantly—confidential. She didn't try to fix me; she simply walked with me. She listened when I needed to speak, sat in silence when words wouldn't come, and reminded me that I wasn't alone. That circle of two saved my life.

This is the season to step out and start **living your healing.** Maybe it's through finding your purpose, helping others, or simply learning how to enjoy life again. You don't have to have it all figured out, but you don't have to do it alone.

the REBUILT WOMAN

Stage 4: The Transformation – A New Beginning

CHAPTER 11
Learning to Trust Again

Trust was something I once gave freely, without hesitation. I believed in the goodness of people, in the promises they made, and in the love they offered. But after the abuse, trust became a distant memory—something I couldn't afford to risk again. I had trusted before, and it had nearly destroyed me. So how could I ever trust again?

The fear wasn't limited to romantic relationships—it extended to friendships, family, even God. I questioned my ability to judge character, to recognize red flags, and to protect myself from being hurt again. Every time someone showed kindness, a voice in my head whispered, What if this is just another mask?

As much as I feared trusting others, I also longed for connection. Isolation had been part of the abuse—keeping me alone, afraid, and dependent. Healing meant breaking free from that isolation, but it also meant confronting the terrifying reality of vulnerability.

Rebuilding Trust, Step by Step

Trust doesn't return all at once. It comes back in small, cautious steps—each one requiring courage, each one testing the wounds that still linger.

Renew My Power

1. Learning to Trust Myself Again Before I could trust anyone else, I had to learn to trust myself—my instincts, my choices, and my ability to walk away when something didn't feel right. The abuse had conditioned me to doubt myself, to silence my intuition. But I came to realize that God had given me discernment for a purpose.

I began by paying closer attention to my gut feelings. If something felt off, I no longer dismissed it. I discovered that my body often sensed danger before my mind could process it. Instead of second-guessing myself, I started to trust that God had planted wisdom deep within me.

I also made peace with myself—for not leaving sooner, for overlooking the warning signs, for loving someone who caused me pain. Self-forgiveness became essential because I couldn't rebuild trust while still holding onto the belief that I was to blame for my past suffering.

2. Trusting God Again One of the most challenging parts of healing was rebuilding my trust in God. I had cried out to Him in my darkest moments— begging for the abuse to stop, for my abuser to change, for a miracle that never came in the way I expected. I questioned whether God had abandoned me, if He had turned His back on my pain.

But as I began to heal, I realized something profound: God had been there all along. He was there in the moments of unexplainable peace that followed nights of chaos. He was there in the strength that carried me through days I didn't think I'd survive. He was there in the people who stepped in to help and the doors that opened when I desperately needed a way out.

I learned to see God not as the one who allowed my suffering, but as the one who rescued me from it. His love had never left me, even when I felt abandoned. And just as I could trust Him to lead me out of the storm, I could trust Him to guide me toward safe and loving relationships.

Psalm 34:18 says, *"The Lord is close to the brokenhearted and saves those who are crushed in spirit."* That verse became my foundation. God was near, and He was restoring me.

3. Trusting Others—Slowly, Wisely

Trusting others again didn't mean blindly opening my heart. It meant learning how to recognize healthy, safe people and building connections with care.

I started small—sharing fragments of my story with friends I sensed were trustworthy. I paid attention to how they responded. Did they listen with compassion? Did they respect my boundaries? Did they offer encouragement without pushing me beyond my comfort zone?

I learned that trust is earned, not freely given. I didn't have to let everyone in. I had the right to take my time, to observe, to set boundaries, and to say no when something didn't feel right. I also came to understand that not everyone in my present was like those who had hurt me in the past. Just because I had been betrayed before didn't mean I was destined to be betrayed again. There were good people in the world—kind, patient, and loving individuals without hidden agendas. Slowly but surely, I began to let them in, one step at a time.

4. Building Healthy Relationships

A crucial part of learning to trust again was understanding what a healthy relationship truly looked like. Abuse had warped my perception of love—I had been conditioned to believe that love meant enduring pain, that apologies could erase harm, and that control was a form of care.

But real love doesn't feel like fear. It doesn't manipulate, control, or make you question your worth. As I healed, I began to see the stark differences between healthy and unhealthy relationships:

- ✅ **Healthy Love:** Respect, patience, honesty, and emotional safety.
- ❌ **Toxic Love:** Control, guilt, manipulation, and fear.

I established a new standard for all my relationships, whether romantic or platonic:
- Consistency over intensity. Love bombing had once deceived me—grand gestures and overwhelming affection that later turned into cruelty. Now, I value steady, genuine kindness over emotional rollercoasters.
- Boundaries are respected, not challenged. Safe people don't push my limits; they honor them.
- I should never feel like I have to shrink myself. Real love lets me be fully seen, fully known, and fully accepted.

5. Embracing Love Again For a long time, I believed love was too risky, too dangerous. But over time, I realized that love itself wasn't the problem—it was who I had chosen to give my love to.

God designed us for connection. He created love to reflect His own heart. And while the enemy had tried to twist and destroy that love in my past, God was faithfully restoring it.

When I finally opened my heart again—to safe friendships, to people who genuinely cared—I rediscovered the beauty of love. I saw that love, when placed in the right hands, could be healing. It could be comforting. It became a glimpse of God's grace, a reminder of His goodness.

Study Spotlight: Post-Traumatic Growth

"Psychologists Tedeschi and Calhoun describe something called post-traumatic growth—where survivors not only recover but discover deeper faith, stronger purpose, and renewed strength after trauma. Pain can become purpose. Your healing journey can open doors you never imagined."
Source: Tedeschi, R. G., & Calhoun, L. G. (1996). The Posttraumatic Growth Inventory: Measuring the positive legacy of trauma. Journal of Traumatic Stress, 9(3), 455–471.

A Letter to the One Who's Afraid to Trust Again

I know what it feels like to be terrified of trusting again. I know the fear that grips your heart, the hesitation, the voice that whispers, What if I get hurt again?

But I want you to know this: Not everyone will hurt you. Not everyone is like the one who broke you.

Take your time. Let trust build slowly. Listen to your instincts, but don't let fear keep you locked away from love. There are safe people out there—people who will see you, cherish you, and never use your past against you.

Most importantly, God is leading you to the right relationships. He is healing your heart, restoring what was broken, and preparing you for a love that is safe and true.

You don't have to trust all at once. You just have to take the first step. And then another. And then another.

One day, you'll realize you're not afraid anymore. You'll realize that love is not something to fear, but something to embrace—wisely, carefully, and with the confidence that you are worthy of it.

Dawn Williams

JOURNAL PROMPT:
Reflection

1. What fears do you have about trusting others again? How can you take small steps toward building healthy relationships?

My Thoughts:

_____
_____
_____
_____
_____
_____
_____
_____
_____

Affirmation: I am allowed to take my time. I will not let fear keep me from experiencing love and connection.

Prayer: God, heal the wounds that make me afraid to trust. Help me to recognize safe, healthy love. Guide me to the right people and protect my heart. Amen.

the REBUILT WOMAN

Stage 4: The Transformation – A New Beginning

CHAPTER 12
Finding My Purpose

From Brokenness to Purpose

There was a time when I thought my story would end in silence—that I would forever live in the shadow of what had been done to me, carrying the weight of my past like an anchor, never truly free. I believed the damage was too deep, the wounds too severe, and the years I had lost were gone forever. But God had other plans.

In the beginning, I couldn't see it. The pain felt meaningless—just an unbearable heaviness pressing on my chest, making it hard to breathe, hard to hope. Grief came in waves: the loss of love, the loss of trust, the loss of the woman I used to be. I wasn't just mourning a relationship; I was mourning the dream I had built around it. Yet, even in my darkest moments, there was a whisper in my spirit: This is not the end.

At first, I didn't understand. How could anything good come from what I had endured? How could a life marked by betrayal, fear, and heartbreak ever be turned into something beautiful? But as I healed—slowly, painfully, intentionally—I began to see the purpose in my pain.

Every tear I cried, every prayer I whispered, every moment I fought to survive—none of it was wasted. God was rebuilding me.

Finding My Purpose

The Psychology of Purpose

From a psychological perspective, purpose is one of the most powerful forces in healing. Research shows that people who find meaning in their suffering often experience post-traumatic growth—where the very pain that tried to break them becomes the foundation for something greater.
Instead of remaining trapped in trauma, they transform.

Viktor Frankl, a Holocaust survivor and psychologist, wrote in *Man's Search for Meaning* that those who survive suffering are the ones who find a deeper purpose beyond their pain. They take what they have endured and use it to fuel something bigger than themselves.

I witnessed this truth unfold in my own life. As I began to share my story—hesitantly at first—I met others who had walked similar paths. Women who carried the same wounds. Women who felt unseen, unheard, and unworthy. In them, I saw a reflection of the woman I had once been.

God was calling me to be the voice I had once needed.

Faith: The Redemption of Pain

One of the most powerful verses that carried me through my healing was **Genesis 50:20:** *"You intended to harm me, but God intended it for good to accomplish what is now being done, the saving of many lives."*

I held onto that promise. What the enemy meant for destruction, God was using for redemption. The pain that once felt like a prison was now becoming the very thing that would set others free.

I started speaking. Writing. Creating safe spaces for women to share their stories. I saw the impact that truth could have—that when we stop hiding in shame, when we bring our pain into the light, healing begins.

And with each step, I realized something profound: My purpose wasn't found in spite of my pain. It was found through it.

Finding My Purpose

Turning Pain Into Power

If you are searching for meaning after trauma, know this: Your pain does not define you, but what you do with it does.

Here's how you can start transforming your wounds into something powerful:

1. **Heal First** – You cannot pour from an empty cup. Before you help others, allow yourself the time and space to heal. Seek therapy, support, and spiritual guidance. Healing is the foundation of purpose.

2. **Find What Sets Your Soul on Fire** – Your story matters, but so does what you do with it. Whether it's advocacy, writing, mentoring, or simply speaking life into someone else—your journey has meaning.

3. **Use Your Voice** – You don't have to stand on a stage to make an impact. A simple conversation, a handwritten letter, a social media post—it all matters. Someone, somewhere, needs to hear your story.

4. **Trust God's Plan** – What feels like the worst chapter of your life might be the very thing God will use to change lives. He doesn't waste pain. He redeems it.

5. **Step Into Boldness** – Fear will try to keep you silent. Shame will tell you that your story isn't worth sharing. But the moment you step into boldness, you reclaim your power.

A Letter to You

A New Dream

I once dreamed of a love that would complete me.
Instead, I found a purpose that fulfilled me.

Now, I dream of a world where survivors rise. Where women who once felt powerless rediscover their strength. Where voices that were once silenced echo with truth and hope.

And I dream of a God who restores.

Because I am living proof that He does.

And so are you.

You are not defined by what happened to you.

You are defined by what you do next.

And I pray that what comes next is the most beautiful chapter yet.

Dawn Williams

JOURNAL PROMPT:

Reflection

1. How has your pain shaped you? What lessons have you learned from your journey that could help others?

My Thoughts:

_____
_____
_____
_____
_____
_____
_____
_____
_____

Affirmation: My story matters. My voice is powerful. My pain is not the end of my story—it is the beginning of something greater.

Prayer:· Lord, take my pain and use it for Your glory. Turn my wounds into wisdom, my suffering into strength. Show me the purpose You have for my life and give me the courage to walk in it. Amen

the REBUILT WOMAN

Stage 4: The Transformation – A New Beginning

CHAPTER 12

A Message to the Woman I Once Was

I remember the nights I cried myself to sleep, wondering if I would ever feel whole again. The days when getting out of bed felt like a battle, and the reflection in the mirror showed a woman I no longer recognized. The weight of shame, the fear that no one would ever understand, and the silence that followed every moment of pain—it was suffocating. If that's where you are right now, I want you to hear me:

You are not alone.

I know it may not feel that way. The enemy will whisper lies, telling you that no one will believe you, that you are too broken, that it was somehow your fault. He wants to keep you trapped in isolation, drowning in shame. But he is a liar. Because the truth is this: You are seen. You are heard. You are worthy.

The pain you carry is not your identity. The abuse you endured is not your future. The darkness that tried to break you will not win. There is a life beyond this—a life filled with peace, joy, and healing. And I promise you, the day will come when you will wake up and realize that the worst parts of your past no longer have power over you.

Faith: The Light in the Darkness

In my darkest moments, when I felt abandoned and unseen, God was there. Even when I questioned Him, even when I doubted His love, He never left me. *"The Lord is close to the brokenhearted and saves those who are crushed in spirit."* — **Psalm 34:18**

I didn't always feel Him, but He was there—in the small moments, in the unexpected kindness of a stranger, in the strength that kept me moving forward when I wanted to give up.

God did not create you to live in fear. He did not bring you into this world to suffer in silence. He has a plan for you—one that is good, one that is filled with hope.

"For I know the plans I have for you," declares the Lord, "plans to prosper you and not to harm you, plans to give you hope and a future." — **Jeremiah 29:11**
Hold onto that truth, even when you can't see it yet. Because healing is coming. Restoration is coming. Freedom is coming.

Study Spotlight: Peer Support

"Research by Goodman and colleagues found that survivors who joined peer-support groups reported greater safety, stronger self-esteem, and deeper healing than those who walked alone. Community matters. Healing is multiplied when we find circles that see us and stand with us."

Source: Goodman, L. A., Smyth, K. F., Borges, A. M., & Singer, R. (2009). When crises collide: How intimate partner violence and poverty intersect to shape women's mental health and coping? Trauma, Violence, & Abuse, 10(4), 306–329.

A Letter to Survivors

To the woman who feels lost, who wonders if she will ever heal, who is still fighting to believe in herself again—this is for you.

You are stronger than you know. The fact that you have survived everything you have been through is proof of that.

You are not defined by what happened to you. You are not broken, you are not unlovable, and you are not to blame. What was done to you does not define your worth.

You are worthy of love. The kind of love that is gentle, kind, and patient. The love that does not hurt or manipulate. But first, you must give that love to yourself.

You are capable of rebuilding. It won't happen overnight, and that's okay. Healing is not a race—it's a journey. One step, one breath, one moment at a time.

You are not alone. There are women—warriors—who have walked this road before you. We stand with you, we believe in you, and we are waiting for you on the other side.

You will rise from this.

You will laugh again.

You will love again.

You will live again.

And when you do, you will see that everything you survived has made you into the woman you were always meant to be.

This is not the end of your story.

This is the beginning of your healing.

You are loved. You are seen. You are never alone.

Dawn Williams

JOURNAL PROMPT:
Reflection

1. If you could speak to your past self—the version of you who was still trapped, still hurting—what would you say to her?

My Thoughts:

_____
_____
_____
_____
_____
_____
_____
_____

Affirmation: I am not alone. I am loved. I am healing. I am stepping into a new, beautiful future.

Prayer: Lord, remind me that I am never alone. When the enemy tries to fill my mind with doubt and fear, replace it with Your truth. Give me strength for today and hope for tomorrow. Lead me into the healing You have promised. In Jesus' name, Amen.

the REBUILT WOMAN

90-Day Scripture Plan for Healing, Strength, and Restoration

Designed to help women recovering from domestic violence grow in faith, overcome trauma, and walk in God's purpose.

This plan is divided into three transformative phases, each focusing on a different aspect of healing:

Phase 1: Healing & Strength (Days 1-30) Overcoming fear, pain, and brokenness.

Phase 2: Rebuilding & Renewing (Days 31-60) Restoring self-worth, breaking free from the past, and walking in freedom.

Phase 3: Walking in Purpose (Days 61-90) Finding joy, embracing God's plan, and stepping into new beginnings.

Each day includes:
- A scripture to anchor your heart in God's Word.
- A reflection to help you process and apply the truth.
- A prayer to guide you in connecting with God.

This plan is designed to walk with you through your healing journey, offering hope, strength, and a renewed sense of purpose.

Renew My Power

90-Day Healing Scripture Plan

📌 **Phase 1: Healing & Strength (Days 1-30)**
(Overcoming fear, pain, and brokenness)

Week 1: God is Your Healer

1. Psalm 147:3 – He heals the brokenhearted and binds up their wounds.
2. Isaiah 41:10 – Do not fear, for I am with you.
3. 2 Timothy 1:7 – God has not given us a spirit of fear.
4. Psalm 34:18 – The Lord is close to the brokenhearted.
5. Exodus 14:14 – The Lord will fight for you; you need only be still.
6. Matthew 11:28 – Come to me, all who are weary, and I will give you rest.
7. Psalm 23:4 – Even though I walk through the darkest valley, I will fear no evil.

Week 2: God's Love & Protection

8. Isaiah 54:17 – No weapon formed against you shall prosper.
9. Romans 8:38-39 – Nothing can separate us from God's love.
10. Psalm 91:4 – He will cover you with His feathers.
11. Deuteronomy 31:8 – The Lord goes before you; He will never leave you.
12. Jeremiah 29:11 – God has plans to prosper you, not harm you.
13. Psalm 46:1 – God is our refuge and strength.
14. Romans 15:13 – May the God of hope fill you with all joy and peace.

Week 3: Releasing the Pain

15. 1 Peter 5:7 – Cast all your anxiety on Him.
16. Isaiah 43:2 – When you pass through the waters, I will be with you.
17. Psalm 55:22 – Cast your burdens on the Lord.
18. John 14:27 – My peace I give you.
19. Lamentations 3:22-23 – His mercies are new every morning.
20. Philippians 4:6-7 – Do not be anxious about anything.
21. Psalm 30:5 – Weeping may endure for a night, but joy comes in the morning.

90-Day Healing Scripture Plan

Week 4: Finding Strength in God

22. Isaiah 40:31 – Those who hope in the Lord will renew their strength.
23. Ephesians 6:10 – Be strong in the Lord and in His mighty power.
24. Nehemiah 8:10 – The joy of the Lord is your strength.
25. 2 Corinthians 12:9 – My grace is sufficient for you.
26. Joshua 1:9 – Be strong and courageous.
27. Psalm 121:1-2 – My help comes from the Lord.
28. Romans 8:28 – In all things, God works for the good of those who love Him.

📌 **Phase 2: Rebuilding & Renewing (Days 31-60)**
(Restoring self-worth, breaking free from the past, and walking in freedom)

Week 5: God Restores Your Identity

29. Genesis 1:27 – You are made in God's image.
30. Psalm 139:14 – You are fearfully and wonderfully made.
31. Ephesians 2:10 – You are God's masterpiece.
32. Galatians 2:20 – Christ lives in you.
33. Romans 8:1 – There is no condemnation for those in Christ.
34. Isaiah 62:3 – You are a crown of beauty in God's hands.
35. 2 Corinthians 5:17 – If anyone is in Christ, they are a new creation.

Week 6: Breaking Free from the Past

36. Isaiah 43:18-19 – Forget the former things; I am doing a new thing.
37. John 8:36 – Whom the Son sets free is free indeed.
38. Romans 12:2 – Be transformed by the renewing of your mind.
39. Galatians 5:1 – Stand firm in the freedom Christ has given you.
40. Hebrews 12:1-2 – Let us throw off everything that hinders.
41. Philippians 3:13-14 – Forgetting what is behind, I press on toward the goal.
42. Ezekiel 36:26 – I will give you a new heart and a new spirit.

90-Day Healing Scripture Plan

Week 7: Walking in God's Peace

43. Colossians 3:15 – Let the peace of Christ rule in your hearts.
44. Isaiah 26:3 – He will keep you in perfect peace.
45. Psalm 37:4 – Delight yourself in the Lord.
46. Zephaniah 3:17 – The Lord your God is with you.
47. Matthew 6:33 – Seek first His kingdom and righteousness.
48. 1 John 4:18 – Perfect love casts out fear.
49. Proverbs 3:5-6 – Trust in the Lord with all your heart.

📌 **Phase 3: Walking in Purpose (Days 61-90)**
(Finding joy, embracing God's plan, and stepping into new beginnings)

Week 8: Embracing Your Calling

50. Jeremiah 1:5 – Before I formed you, I knew you.
51. Matthew 5:14 – You are the light of the world.
52. Proverbs 31:25 – She is clothed with strength and dignity.
53. 2 Corinthians 1:3-4 – God comforts us so we can comfort others.
54. 1 Peter 2:9 – You are chosen, royal, and God's special possession.
55. Isaiah 60:1 – Arise, shine, for your light has come.
56. Mark 16:15 – Go into all the world and preach the gospel.

Week 9: Finding Joy Again

57. John 15:11 – My joy may be in you.
58. Psalm 126:5 – Those who sow in tears will reap in joy.
59. Romans 15:13 – The God of hope will fill you with joy.
60. Psalm 16:11 – In His presence, there is fullness of joy.
61. Habakkuk 3:18 – Yet I will rejoice in the Lord.
62. Philippians 4:4 – Rejoice in the Lord always.
63. Psalm 118:24 – This is the day the Lord has made; let us rejoice.

How to Use This Plan

- **·Read & Reflect** – Spend time meditating on the scripture.
- **·Pray** – Speak God's promises over your life.
- **·Journal – Write how each verse applies to your journey.**
- **·Declare** – Speak affirmations based on these scriptures daily.

Support Resources

Domestic violence (DV) support resources, including hotlines, shelters, legal aid, and therapy options. These resources are specific to Australia, but I'll also include some general global options.

Australia:

1. 1800RESPECT

National Sexual Assault, Domestic Family Violence Counselling Service
- Phone: 1800 737 732 (24/7)
- Website: https://www.1800respect.org.au
- Online chat and resources for safety planning, counseling, and referrals.
- Domestic Violence Resource Service (DVRS) Phone: 07 5591 2956 (Gold Coast)
- Website: https://www.dvrs.org.au
- Provides support, legal advice, and crisis accommodation for women.

2. QLD Domestic Violence Hotline
- Phone: 1800 811 811
- Provides support and crisis intervention for those experiencing DV in Queensland.

3. Women's Legal Service Queensland
- Phone: 1800 957 957
- Website: https://www.wlsq.org.au
- Provides free legal advice and support for women affected by domestic violence.

4. The National Domestic Violence Order Scheme (NDVOS)
- Provides protection across Australia with information on how to access DV orders and legal protection across state borders.

5. Brisbane Domestic Violence Service (BDVS)
- Phone: 07 3217 2544
- Provides support services, including case management, counseling, and referrals.

6. **Lifeline Australia**
   - Phone: 13 11 14
   - Website: https://www.lifeline.org.au
   - Offers crisis support and suicide prevention services, available 24/7.
7. **Child Protection and Family Support (Queensland)**
   - Phone: 13 12 78
   - Website: https://www.communities.qld.gov.au
   - Provides support for children and families facing abuse.
8. **Legal Aid Queensland**
   - Phone: 1300 65 11 88
   - Website: https://www.legalaid.qld.gov.au
   - Offers legal assistance, including for domestic violence-related matters.

Global Resources

1. **National Domestic Violence Hotline (USA)**
   - Phone: 1-800-799-SAFE (7233)
   - Website: https://www.thehotline.org
   - Provides confidential support, resources, and safety planning in the U.S.
2. **Refuge (UK)**
   - Website: https://www.refuge.org.uk
   - Offers support to women and children experiencing domestic violence.
3. **Shelter (UK)**
   - Phone: 0808 800 4444
   - Website: https://www.shelter.org.uk
   - Provides housing and shelter support for those fleeing domestic violence.
4. **The Canadian Women's Foundation**
   - Website: https://www.canadianwomen.org
   - Offers resources for women facing abuse and support for those fleeing violence.

Therapy and Counselling Options

1. Counselling Services (Australia)
   - The Australian Counselling Association (ACA)
   - Website: https://www.counsellingaustralia.com.au
   - Provides a directory of registered counselors for trauma and domestic violence recovery.

2. **Therapists Specializing in Trauma Therapy with Dawn - Gold Coast**

3. **Group Therapy and Support Groups:**

Join The Rebuilt Woman Healing Circle (Face to Face or Online)

Reclaim Your Strength, Rediscover Your Peace

The Rebuilt Movement- Together We Heal

Are you a woman recovering from domestic violence, abuse, or betrayal? You're not alone. The Rebuilt Movement - Healing circles is a safe space where you can heal, grow, and rebuild your life with the support of a compassionate community.

In our The Rebuilt Movement, you'll receive:

- **Empowerment:** Through emotional support and practical tools for healing.
- **Group Therpy:** Sharing & Healing together
- **Connection:** A sisterhood of women who understand your journey and walk beside you.
- **Faith-Based and Psychological Healing:** A unique blend of spiritual and psychological guidance for complete restoration.
- **Confidentiality and Safety:** A trusted environment where you can share, learn, and heal at your own pace.

It's time to start your journey towards healing, peace, and freedom. Join The Rebuilt Woman Healing Circle today.

For more information and to sign up & register here:

You are worthy of a rebuilt life—come, let us walk with you.

The Invitation

Next Steps:

Join the Movement — Your Journey Begins Here

You've bravely walked through these pages, and now a new chapter is waiting for you. You don't have to rebuild alone. You're invited into a community of women rising, healing, and leading together.
This is more than a book.
This is a movement.

Free Online Support — The Rebuilt Series TV (YouTube)
Access weekly videos, healing tools, conversations, and guidance to support your emotional and relational growth.

Become a Rebuilt Woman Volunteer & Facilitator
After you've progressed on your healing journey, you may feel called to help others. *Register your interest here:*

For anything else visit the Website
Find where Dawn is speaking, books, products, healing circle & event dates, facilitator training, survivor resources, and everything connected to the movement:
www.therebuiltwoman.com

We're here to support you every step of the way. Scan the QR codes today to begin your journey toward healing and transformation.

Recommended Reading

- Patrick Carnes – The Betrayal Bond

A powerful book that explains trauma bonding and why people stay in destructive relationships.

- CDC & Kaiser Permanente – The ACE Study

A Groundbreaking research showing how childhood abuse and family dysfunction shape adult health and relationships.

- Lenore Walker – The Battered Woman

Classic research that introduced the idea of the "cycle of violence" in abusive relationships.

- Adams et al. – Economic Abuse Study

Research revealing that nearly all survivors experience financial abuse and control.

- Jacquelyn Campbell – Danger Assessment

Research showing the first two weeks after leaving are the most dangerous time for survivors.

- J. M. Golding – Intimate Partner Violence & PTSD

A meta-analysis showing high rates of PTSD among survivors, often higher than combat veterans.

- Kenneth Pargament – The Psychology of Religion and Coping

A comprehensive look at how faith and spirituality support healing and resilience.

- Goodman et al. – Peer Support and Mental Health

Research showing that healing is stronger and longer-lasting when survivors have supportive communities.

- Kitzmann et al. – Children's Recovery Study

Evidence that children exposed to violence can heal and thrive with safe environments and support.

- Tedeschi & Calhoun – Post-Traumatic Growth

Research showing how trauma survivors can grow stronger, discover deeper faith, and live with renewed purpose.

The Rebuilt Series

Your Rebuild Has Only Just Begun

If this book reached you, it's because a part of you was ready — ready to break cycles, reclaim your voice, and choose yourself again. But this is only the first step. The Rebuilt Series guides you through every layer of your transformation: mind, heart, soul, identity, purpose, leadership, and legacy.

BOOK 2: THE REBUILT SOUL – GOLD EDITION

Why You Should Keep Going
Trauma may have cracked you, but it never destroyed you.

Just like Kintsugi mends broken pottery with gold, every healed place in your story becomes a place of strength and beauty.

The Rebuilt Soul takes you deeper into:
- The 12 Transitional Healings every woman must walk through
- Breaking generational patterns with clarity
- Rebuilding identity, boundaries, and self-worth
- Strengthening emotional, mental, and relational foundations
- Creating a life that feels grounded, peaceful, and aligned

This next book invites you to pick up the gold and rebuild the part of you that still hopes, still believes, and still longs for more.

WHAT'S COMING NEXT IN THE SERIES:

Book 1 – Emerald: The Rebuilt Woman- Identity, confidence, voice, inner strength.
Book 2 – Gold: The Rebuilt Soul- Heart work, emotional repair, generational change.
Book 3 – Onyx: The Rebuilt Leader- Power, purpose, leadership, wealth.
Book 4 – Diamond: The Rebuilt Legacy- Wisdom, relationships, motherhood, generational healing.

Together, these books create a complete transformation journey for the woman who refuses to remain broken.

Plus –The Rebuilt Man — Iron Edition

A bold, compassionate exploration into the healing of men — their hidden battles, their silent wounds, and the fire that forges them into leaders, protectors, and legacy builders.

KEEP WALKING — YOUR STORY IS STILL BEING REBUILT

If something awakened in you through this book, trust it.
Your next chapter is calling you forward — and you are more ready than you know.
Become the rebuilt woman you were born to be.

REBUILD YOUR MIND.
RESTORE YOUR BODY.
RENEW YOUR STRENGTH.

THE REBUILT WOMAN™ HEALTH RANGE
Daily Vitality Formula

REBUILD YOUR MIND + BODY

AVAILABLE ONLINE
WWW.THEREBUILTWOMAN.COM.AU

SCAN ME! ORDER

www.ingramcontent.com/pod-product-compliance
Lightning Source LLC
Chambersburg PA
CBHW071326080526
44587CB00018B/3360